Daily Discoveries
for November

Thematic Learning Activities for
EVERY DAY

Written by Elizabeth Cole Midgley

Illustrated by Jennette Guymon-King

Teaching & Learning Company

1204 Buchanan St., P.O. Box 10
Carthage, IL 62321-0010

This book belongs to

_____

Cover art by Jennette Guymon-King

Copyright © 2005, Teaching & Learning Company

ISBN No. 1-57310-464-7

Printing No. 987654321

Teaching & Learning Company
1204 Buchanan St., P.O. Box 10
Carthage, IL 62321-0010

Several of the activities in this book invove preparing, tasting and sharing food items. We urge you to be aware of any food allergies or restrictions your students may have and to supervise these activities diligently. All food-related suggestions are identified with this allergy-alert symbol: ⚠

Please note: small food items (candies, raisins, cereal, etc.) can also pose a choking hazard.

At the time of publication every effort was made to insure the accuracy of the information included in this book. However, we cannot guarantee that agencies and organizations mentioned will continue to operate or maintain these current locations.

Table of Contents

Dear Teacher or Parent,

Due to the stimulus of a high-tech world, parents and teachers are often faced with the challenge of how to capture the attention of a child and create an atmosphere of meaningful learning opportunities. Often we search for new ways to meet this challenge and help young people transfer their knowledge, skills and experiences from one area to another. Subjects taught in isolation can leave a feeling of fragmentation. More and more educators are looking for ways to be able to integrate curriculum so that their students can fully understand how things relate to each other.

The Daily Discoveries series has been developed to that end. The premise behind this series has been, in part, the author's educational philosophy: anything can be taught and absorbed by others in a meaningful way, depending upon its presentation.

In this series, each day has been researched around the history of a specific individual or event and has been developed into a celebration or theme with integrated curriculum areas. In this approach to learning students draw from their own experience and understanding of things, to a level of processing new information and skills.

The Daily Discoveries series is an almanac-of-sorts, 12 books (one for each month) that present a thematically based curriculum for grades K-6. The series contains hundreds and hundreds of resources and ideas that can be a natural springboard to learning. These ideas have been used in the classroom and at home, and are fun as well as educationally sound. The activities have been endorsed by professors, teachers, parents and, best of all, by children.

The Daily Discoveries series can be used in the following ways for school or home:
- to develop new skills and reinforce previous learning
- to create a sense of fun and celebration every day
- as tutoring resources
- as enrichment activities that can be used as time allows
- for family fun activities

Sincerely,

Elizabeth

Elizabeth Cole Midgley

National Author's Day

November 1

Setting the Stage

• Set up a carpenter's area (with carpenter apron, tools and blue-prints) and a bulletin board with the caption: "A Writer's Tools." Put tools on the board with labels such as: Main Idea, Personal Voice, Description and Details, Sensory Imagery, Vocabulary and Word Choice.

Historical Background

A famous American author, Stephen Crane, was born on this date in 1871. He wrote the book, *The Red Badge of Courage.*

Literary Exploration

Author's Day by Daniel Manus Pinkwater
Books Are by People by Lee Bennett Hopkins
Dear Mr. Henshaw by Beverly Cleary
How a Book Is Made by Aliki
A Writer Begins by Clyde Robert Bulla

Language Experience

• Begin reading *Dear Mr. Henshaw,* by Beverly Cleary. Encourage students to finish the book to see what happens next.

• Discuss what makes a good book. What tools must an author have to be able to write books? How does an author get his or her ideas?

• Share biographical sketches of several different authors.

Writing Experience

• Discuss writing tools, author's style and patterns, importance of mechanics (capitalization, punctuation, indention and correct spelling). Post these questions on a bulletin board:

Does it make sense?

Does it have a beginning, middle and end?

Does it have a main idea?

Is there proper capitalization?

Are punctuation marks used in the right places?

• Write a letter to a favorite author. Send the letter to the author's publisher with a stamped, self-addressed envelope.

• Let the students author their own "published" stories/books to put in a class library for others to read.

• Set up a "treasure chest" (shoe box) filled with story starters to turn your children on to writing books! See patterns on page 8 for decorating your treasure chest.

Story starter ideas:

My Best Friend	My Favorite Trip
The Time I Got Lost	My Favorite Birthday
My Happiest Moment	One time I got so mad . . .
I opened the door and saw . . .	This animal . . .
More fun than bubble gum is . . .	What Is a Mother?
Snow is . . .	Love is . . .
What Is a Father?	As beautiful as . . .
As happy as . . .	Describe yourself
As slippery as . . .	If I Were a Bird
My Life in a Doghouse	One Windy Night
My Trip to the Dentist	My Summer Travels
The Night the Electricity Went Off	The World in 2050
If I Were a Football	The Substitute Teacher
The New Theme Park Attraction	The First Day of School
The funniest time I ever had was . . .	How to Build a Snowman
Secrets from a Secret Agent	The Most Unusual Recipe
Our Favorite Family Story	My Parents Were So Proud
The Unexpected Guest Under My Bed	So far I'm learning about . . .
My Favorite Teacher	

6

Math Experience

• Allow students time to survey other classmates about their favorite authors. (You might want to display several books.) Tally the results and show them on a class bar graph.

Social Studies Experience

• Have kids imagine the kind of book they might like to write someday. Have them write their biographies to go on the book jackets. Let them exchange papers and guess which book "bio" belongs to whom.

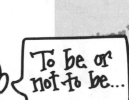

Music/Dramatic Experience

• Dress as a favorite author.

• Describe or illustrate the process an author has to go through to get a book ready for publication.

• Let the students role-play favorite authors. Pair each "author" with a student interviewer to find out what he or she wrote. Have the "author" explain the inspiration for writing that book.

• Let all students pretend to be authors and try to "sell" or advertise their new books so others will want to buy and read them.

Extension Activities

• Invite a local author to visit your class.

• Visit a local bookbindery.

⚠ Make books children can really sink their teeth into. Give each one two graham crackers and frosting. Have them spread the frosting between the two crackers to make edible "books."

• Display a variety of books by different authors. Encourage students to read the biographies on the back covers and share their discoveries.

• Set up an "Author's Chair" where students can share stories they have written with an audience.

Glue to
← lid side

Glue to
corners
of box →

← Glue to
box side

Writing Treasures

Daniel Boone's Birthday

November 2

Setting the Stage

• Display forts and cabins made of Lincoln Logs™.

• Display books about the 18th century.

Historical Background

Daniel Boone was an American pioneer born on this day in 1734.

Daniel
Boone

Literary Exploration

Daniel Boone by Esther Holden Averill
Daniel Boone by James Daugherty
Daniel Boone by Jan Gleiter
Daniel Boone by Laurie Lawlor
Daniel Boone in the Wilderness by Matthew Grant
Daniel Boone: In the Wilderness by Dan Zadra
Daniel Boone: Man of the Forests by Carol Greene
Daniel Boone: Pioneer Trailblazer by Jim Hargrove
Daniel Boone, Taming of the Wilds by Katharine Elliott Wilkie
Daniel Boone: Young Hunter and Tracker by Augusta Stevenson
Daniel Boone's Echo by William Owen Steele
Frontier Living by Edwin Tunis
Let's Be Early Settlers with Daniel Boone by Peggy Parish
The Story of Daniel Boone by William Owen Steele
The Story of Daniel Boone, Wilderness Explorer by Walter Retan
When I Was Young in the Mountains by Cynthia Rylant

Daniel
Boone

Writing Experience

• Have students inscribe their name or message on a "tree" sample.

Daniel
Boone

Daniel
Boone

Social Studies Experience

• Incorporate map-making skills by having students map out an area with familiar landmarks.

Daniel
Boone

Music/Dramatic Experience

• Sing the old familiar tune "Skip to My Lou."

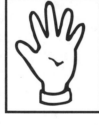

Physical/Sensory Experience

• Play pioneer or frontier games such as: Red Rover, Hide and Seek or Hopscotch.

• Make homemade soap candles.

Daniel
Boone

Arts/Crafts Experience

- Make a frontier cap from a small brown paper bag. Cut off the top half of the bag, then cut strips for fringe all around it. Turn it upside down. Cut a "tail" out of the remaining brown bag fringe. Staple the "tail" to the back of the cap.

Extension Activities

⚠ Make Johnny Cake and serve it with homemade butter.

Johnny Cake

1 c. cornmeal
1/2 t. baking soda
1 t. cream of tartar
1/4 t. salt

Combine the above then add:
1/4 c. honey
1 T. molasses
1 T. melted butter
1 c. milk
1 beaten egg

Put in greased 8" pan. Bake at 425°F for about 25 minutes. Serve with homemade butter.

- Students can make log cabins by sticking pretzels to a milk carton. Use white frosting for "glue."

- Check your local area for pioneer museums or landmarks to visit. Let students make observational drawings.

National Sandwich Day

November 3

Setting the Stage
- Display sandwich ingredients.

Historical Background

John Montague, Earl of Sandwich, was born on this date in 1718. He is credited with the invention of the sandwich (though Romans had also put meat between two slices of bread). The Earl of Sandwich did not want to be interrupted for a meal between card games, so he asked a servant to put the meat between slices of bread so he could continue playing.

Literary Exploration

The Giant Jam Sandwich by John Vernon Lord
The Giant Sandwich by Seth Agnew
I Gave Thomas Edison My Sandwich by Floyd Moore
The King of Prussia and a Peanut Butter Sandwich by Alice Fleming
The Meat in the Sandwich by Alice Bach
The Mother's Day Sandwich by Jillian Wynot
"Recipe for a Hippopotamus Sandwich" by Shel Silverstein (poem from
        Where the Sidewalk Ends)
Sam's Sandwich by David Pelham

Language Experience

⚠️ Have a student tell how to make a favorite sandwich. Another student should make it following the description. Talk about the importance of giving specific directions and following them exactly. (Example: If the directions say to put the peanut butter on the bread, the jar of peanut butter can be placed on the bread.)

Writing Experience

• Write a story from the sandwich's point of view.

• Make "sandwich" books. On two paper slices of bread, a piece of cheese, lettuce and tomato, have students write a story or retell a sequence of a story for a book report. Staple the pages together. See patterns on pages 16 and 17.

• Have students write steps for making a peanut butter sandwich. This is a wonderful way to teach sequencing skills. Use the reproducible on page 18.

Example:
1. Get a jar of peanut butter.
2. Get out two slices of bread.
3. Get out a knife.
4. Take a large glob of peanut butter from the jar and spread it all over one side of the bread.
5. Put the other slice of bread on top of the peanut butter and eat!

How to make a **peanut butter** sandwich

1.
2.
3.
4.
5.
6.
7.
8.
9.
10.

Name:

Sandwich Day

Sandwich Day

andwich Day

Math Experience

• Make up sandwich story problems. Give each sandwich item a monetary amount (lettuce-5 cents, ham-8 cents, etc.) Ask students to compile their ingredients to form a sandwich and add the total price. (Example: Dan wanted to buy a ham and cheese sandwich. He only had 35 cents in his pocket. Can he afford to buy one?)

• Make a bar graph of favorite kinds of sandwiches. Let students draw and cut out favorite ingredients and place them on a bar graph.

Science/Health Experience

⚠ Create healthy sandwiches from nutritional ingredients (the major food groups). See the reproducible on page 19.

Our Favorite Sandwich

❑ Peanut Butter & Jelly
❑ Turkey
❑ Ham
❑ Tuna Fish
❑ Gilled Cheese
❑ Chicken

Our class picked

_____

as our favorite sandwich!
My family's favorite
sandwich is

_____

Can you create a sandwich
from all four food groups?

Dairy _____   Bread _____

Meat _____   Fruits/Vegetables _____

Name:

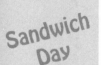

Social Studies Experience

⚠ Invite students to bring their favorite sandwiches and exchange them with one another.

• Discuss different cultures in other places around the world and the kinds of sandwiches they might eat.

Music/Dramatic Experience

- Introduce the old-time "sandwich board" advertising. Let students design two giant signs on poster board to advertise their favorite sandwiches. Punch holes in the top of each poster and add straps of heavy yarn. Let students hang their posters over their shoulders to advertise their particular sandwiches.

Physical/Sensory Experience

- Have students "invent" a new type of sandwich.

Extension Activities

⚠ Make an "accordion" sandwich loaf by slicing one-inch cuts (not all the way through) along a loaf of French bread. After spreading mayonnaise in the cut areas, place meat and cheese slices in each opening.

⚠ Make open-faced sandwiches and add facial features with olives, raisins, pickles, or fruit slices.

⚠ After reading *The Giant Jam Sandwich* by John Vernon Lord, make a giant sandwich. Slice a large loaf of French bread through the middle. Let the students spread on jam and place raisins (for insects) on top of the jam. Put the top of the loaf back on, divide it up and enjoy!

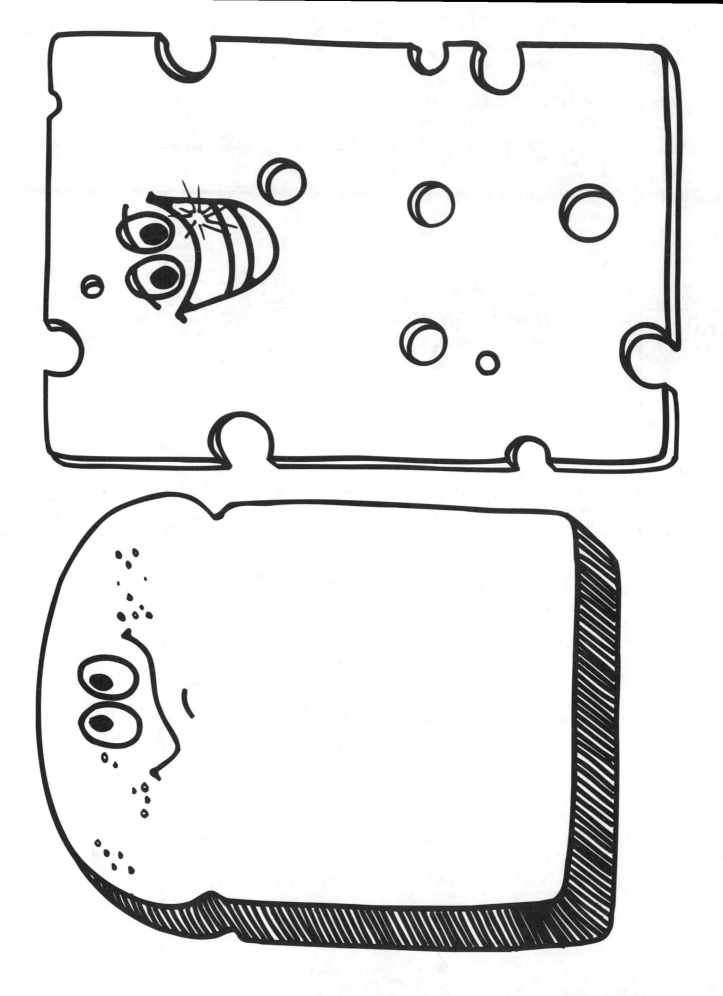

How to make a peanut butter sandwich

1.
2.
3.
4.
5.
6.
7.
8.
9.
10.

Name:

Our Favorite Sandwich

- ☐ Peanut Butter & Jelly
- ☐ Turkey
- ☐ Ham
- ☐ Tuna Fish
- ☐ Gilled Cheese
- ☐ Chicken

Our class picked

_____

as our favorite sandwich!

My family's favorite

sandwich is

_____

Can you create a sandwich
from all four food groups?

Dairy _____   Bread _____

Meat _____   Fruits/Vegetables _____

Name:

Pilgrims' Pride Day

November 4

Setting the Stage

- Display books or book jackets around an ocean background with a paper *Mayflower* ship heading towards the books, or pin book jackets to the ship's sails with the caption: "Take a Trip of Your Own to . . . ."

- Place a large paper *Mayflower* ship between textured paper waves. Let students draw paper doll figures of Pilgrims and Indians aboard the ship waving. The clouds can contain the caption: "Mayflower Memories."

- Draw a full-size pilgrim costume on paper, cut it out and attach it to a full-length mirror. Students can stand in front of the mirror to see how they might have looked in 1620.

Historical Background

In order to worship as they pleased, a group of men, women and children set sail on a ship called the *Mayflower* for a new land. They survived hardships and began their new life in what we now call America.

Literary Exploration

Coming of the Pilgrims by E. Brooks Smith

Cranberry Thanksgiving by Wende Devlin

Eating the Plates: A Pilgrim Book of Food and Manners by Lucille Penner

Fur Trappers and Traders: The Indians, The Pilgrims, and the Beaver by Beatrice Siegel

How Many Days to America?: A Thanksgiving Story by Eve Bunting

If You Lived in Colonial Times by Ann McGovern

If You Sailed on the Mayflower by Ann McGovern

John Alden and the Pilgrim Cow by Margaret Friskey

The Landing of the Pilgrims by James Daugherty

Merrily Comes Our Harvest In: Poems for Thanksgiving by Lee Bennett Hopkins

Molly's Pilgrim by Barbara Cohen

A New Look at the Pilgrims: Why They Came to America by Beatrice Siegel

Peanut Butter Pilgrims by Judy Delton

Pilgrim Children Come to Plymouth by Ida DeLage

Pilgrim Courage, from a First-Hand Account by William Bradford

Pilgrim Neighbors by Elvajean Hall

Pilgrim Stories by Elvajean Hall

Pilgrim Thanksgiving by Wilma Hays

The Pilgrim's First Thanksgiving by Ann McGovern

The Pilgrims' Party: A Really Truly Story by Sadyebeth Lowitz

The Pilgrim's Progress in Modern English by John Bunyan

The Pilgrims of Plymouth by Marcia Sewell

The Plymouth Thanksgiving by Leonard Weisgard

Samuel Eaton's Day: A Day in the Life of a Pilgrim Boy by Kate Waters

Sarah Morton's Story: A Day in the Life of a Pilgrim Girl by Kate Waters

The Thanksgiving Story by Alice Dagliesh

Three Young Pilgrims by Cheryl Harness

Turkeys, Pilgrims and Indian Corn: The Story of the Thanksgiving Symbols by Edna Barth

Year of the Pilgrims by Genevieve Foster

Language Experience

• How many words can you make from the letters in the word *Pilgrim*?

• Put together a book sequencing the events surrounding the Pilgrims' voyage.

Writing Experience

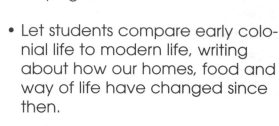

- If students could only pack one chest with their family belongings to make the voyage across the ocean, what would they take? (Remind them that they would need things to start a whole new life: seeds, shovel, etc.) Have them write on the reproducible on page 26.

- Let students compare early colonial life to modern life, writing about how our homes, food and way of life have changed since then.

- Challenge students to divide a sheet of paper into four sections and write on each something a child might do today contrasted with what a child might have done in colonial days. You may prefer to have them write in each section one of the following: chores, play, food and dress.

- Ask each student to write about how the Pilgrims and Indians helped each other.

- Let children each write a story about a Pilgrim boy or girl and paste it to a Pilgrim hat.

- Have students describe their reactions stepping off the *Mayflower*. Use this story starter: "I heard about America and wanted to go, but when I stepped off the *Mayflower* I never thought I'd see . . . ."

Writing Experience continued

- Have students write their feelings in a journal entry as if they had just come to a new country. See reproducible on page 27.

- Let students write letters to old friends back in England, explaining about life in the Plymouth Colony.

How would I feel if I had just arrived in the **NEW COUNTRY?**

Name:

Math Experience

- It took 66 days for the Pilgrims to make their voyage. Let students estimate what the travel time would be today with modern traveling methods.

- Find out how large the *Mayflower* ship was and measure it out in string. Lay the string out in a *Mayflower* shape. Estimate how many people could comfortably sit in that space.

Social Studies Experience

- On a map, trace the journey the Pilgrims made across the ocean.

- Research key figures such as, Governor William Bradford, Miles Standish or Chief Massasoit and the roles they played in early American history.

Music/Dramatic Experience

- Act out the Pilgrim voyage and arrival in the New World.

Physical/Sensory Experience

• Play games Pilgrim children might have played: "Here We Go 'Round the Mulberry Bush," Hide and Seek, tag or marbles.

Arts/Crafts Experience

• Let students make a mural scene depicting the Pilgrims making their journey across the ocean.

• Make pilgrim costumes to wear.

• Aprons for the girls can be made out of white drawstring garbage bags slit in half.

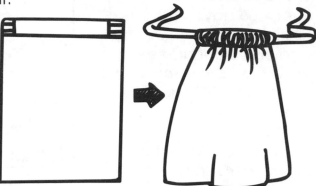

• A collar for girls can be made from a 12" x18" sheet of white construction paper. After folding the paper in half, cut a large circle in the center. Cut a notch to the center to enable students to put it around the neck.

• A boy's Pilgrim hat can be made by folding a large sheet of black construction paper in half. Trace a hat shape on the fold. Cut a slit across it to fit on the head.

TLC10464 Copyright © Teaching & Learning Company, Carthage, IL 62321-0010

Arts/Crafts Experience continued

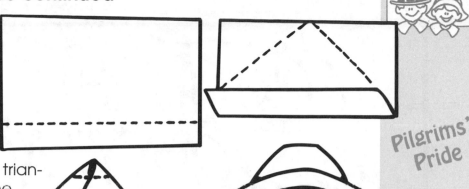

- A pilgrim hat for girls can be made from a 12" x 18" sheet of white paper. Fold it up about 1¹/₂" lengthwise from the edge. Bring both corners down and staple them to form a triangle. Fold the top of the triangle down about another inch and staple it.

- Make a 3-D *Mayflower* ship scene by stapling blue waves together at the sides. Set the cut-off bottom of a small milk carton inside for the ship. Add paper sails secured with straws to a blob of clay.

- Make a *Mayflower* ship from a walnut shell half. Place a small lump of clay in the bottom and stick in a toothpick with a rectangular paper sail attached to it.

- Have students make chest-shaped boxes and "pack" them for their voyage with cut-out magazine pictures of items they want to take.

Extension Activities

⚠ Make cranberry sauce (Pilgrim-style):

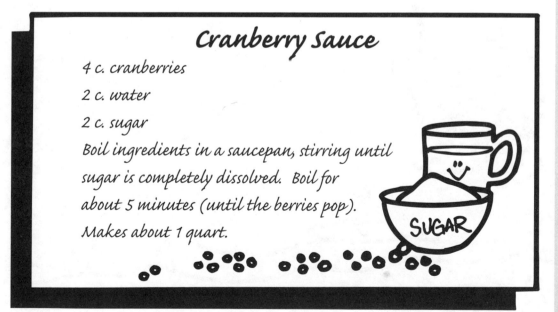

Cranberry Sauce

4 c. cranberries

2 c. water

2 c. sugar

Boil ingredients in a saucepan, stirring until sugar is completely dissolved. Boil for about 5 minutes (until the berries pop). Makes about 1 quart.

⚠ Serve some dried apples, pears or berries as the Pilgrims ate to survive the harsh winter months.

MY OCEAN VOYAGE

If I could only pack one chest of belongings, what would I take?

Name:

How would I feel if I had just arrived in the NEW COUNTRY?

Name:

American Art Day

November 5

Setting the Stage

- Set up your room like an artist's studio. Display art samples, mediums, an artist's paint palette, a French beret, paintbrush and an easel with various samples to promote interest.

- Display student artwork on the board with the caption: "Our Art Gallery Masterpieces."

- If messes are a concern, drape a plastic tablecloth on the floor and call the area, "Artist Island." Encourage students to bring art smocks or oversized old shirts to wear when painting.

Literary Exploration

Adventures of Three Colors by Annette Tison
Alexander Calder and His Magical Mobiles by Jean Lipman
The Art Lesson by Tomie de Paola
The Art of the New American Nation by Shirley Glubok
The Artist by John Bianchi
Bear's Picture by Daniel Pinkwater
Begin at the Beginning by Amy Schwartz
Children in Art by Kate Sedgwick
Drawing from Nature by Jim Arnosky
Drawn from New England: Tasha Tudor by Bethany Tudor
Ed Emberley's Big Orange Drawing Book by Ed Emberley
From the Hills of Georgia by Mattie Lou O'Kelley
History of Art by Marshall Davidson
Just Imagine: Ideas in Painting by Robert Cummings
The Magic of Color by Hilda Simon
Norman the Doorman by Don Freeman
The Pantheon Story of American Art for Young People by Ariane Batterberry
Turnabout, Think About, Look About Book by Beau Gardner

TLC10464 Copyright © Teaching & Learning Company, Carthage, IL 62321-0010

Writing Experience

• Discuss and write about art—what it is and who determines its value. Discuss how there are no rules or right or wrong ways to be an artist. Talk about how we can show our personality through our artwork.

• Let students write about how they feel when they express themselves through art.

• Ask each student to imagine he or she is one of the greatest artists in America. Have them write descriptions of their masterpieces and tell how they were able to create them.

• Students can decorate stationery for letters to their favorite American artists. Stamps, glitter markers, press-on letters or stickers can be used.

• Let students write stories about famous American paintings.

• See reproducible for writing activities on page 33.

Math Experience

• Have an art gallery showing. Let students price their artwork, then give them play money. Let them figure out if they can afford to purchase other students' artwork. See Art Bucks patterns on page 34.

Science/Health Experience

• Experiment with different colors on student palettes. Decide which ones might be considered warm and cool colors.

Social Studies Experience

• Show art prints, books or slides by artists throughout American history.

Music/Dramatic Experience

• Have a student pose as an artist model with different angles and expressions while other students draw or paint what they see.

• Let students "advertise" their paintings to sell them.

• Divide students into two teams for a mini debate on what constitutes great art.

Physical/Sensory Experience

• Have students draw or paint as you play musical selections. Change the mood by changing the tempo of the music.

Arts/Crafts Experience

- Provide art supplies such as paper, paint, crayons, clay, easels or craft items for free-time creations.

- Let students make sculptures of themselves from clay, wire or wood.

- Have students create their own works of architecture from rolled or folded paper, tubes, straws, toothpicks, foam pieces, scrap wood or pipe cleaners.

- Cover a table with butcher paper to make a "Doodle Table." Let students create on it as time permits.

- Let them decorate white T-shirts with puff-paint or glitter markers.

- Draw around students' bodies with markers and let them add features and clothes.

- Provide students with hand mirrors and let them draw self-portraits.

- Challenge students to make collages of odd scraps or craft materials.

American
Art Day

American
Art Day

American
Art Day

Extension Activities

• Visit a local art museum.

• Invite local artists to pay your class a visit to share their passion for art, give examples of ideas or demonstrate their special technique.

• Order posters from the Metropolitan Museum of Art.

⚠ Let students get one another's autographs before anyone becomes famous. Make "Signature Cinnamon Slices" by toasting bread, then letting students dribble liquid margarine on it in the shape of their signatures. Sprinkle a little cinnamon sugar on top for a delicious treat!

Follow-Up/Homework Idea

• Have students research American artists such as: Georgia O'Keeffe, Mary Cassatt, Andy Warhol, Andrew Wyeth or Winslow Homer and report their findings.

32

Name:

John Philip Sousa's Birthday

November 6

Setting the Stage
• Display student work and pictures of instruments with the caption: "Our Work Is Darn Tootin'."

Historical Background
John Philip Sousa was an American composer and bandleader famous for such tunes as "Stars and Stripes Forever." He was born on this date in 1854 in Washington, D.C. He was known as "The March King."

Literary Exploration
Brother Billy Bronto's Bygone Blues Band by David Birchman
Gator and Mary's Traveling Band by David Martin
Grandma's Band by Brad Bowles
The Happy Hedgehog Band by Martin Waddell
Homemade Band by Hap Palmer
John Philip Sousa: The March King by Carol Greene
The Little Band by James Sage
Make Your Own Musical Instruments by Margaret McLean
Musical Instruments by Alan Blackwood
"Orchestra" a poem from *Where the Sidewalk Ends* by Shel Silverstein
Picture Book of Musical Instruments by Marion Lacey
Rhythms, Music and Instruments to Make by John Hawkinson
Ty's One-Man Band by Mildred Pitts Walter

Writing Experience

• Write a story about the night of the big concert when you began to play your instrument and no sound came out. See reproducible on page 38.

Social Studies Experience

• Research the history of early American musical instruments.

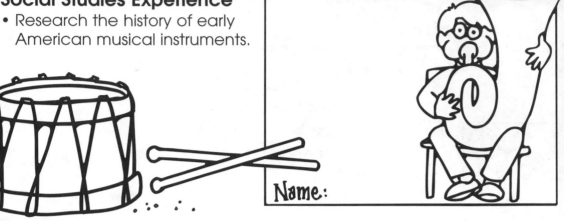

Night of the **BIG CONCERT**

Name:

Music/Dramatic Experience

• Talk about band instruments and their sounds.

• Play musical instruments on tape or CD. Have students guess the instruments.

• Teach students simple techniques in leading music. Let them try leading each other playing imaginary instruments.

Physical/Sensory Experience

• Play musical chairs to John Philip Sousa's music.

• Let students march to "Stars and Stripes Forever." One child can carry a flag while the rest pretend to play a favorite musical instrument. Parade around the school or playground.

Arts/Crafts Experience

• Let students make flags to carry in their marching band.

• Have students make homemade instruments. A drum can be made out of an oatmeal box. A tambourine can be made from two paper plates filled with beans, popcorn or bells and stapled together. Humming over a wax paper-covered comb can sound like a harmonica. A pencil can be a percussion instrument. Toilet paper tubes can be bean-filled shakers with paper circles or fabric attached with rubber bands around the ends. Castanets can be made by gluing bottle caps to a folded piece of thick cardboard. Small guitars can be made by stretching rubber bands across empty tissue boxes.

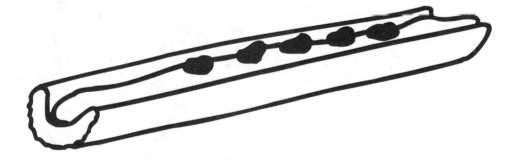

Extension Activities

⚠ Make "flutes" from peanut butter or cream cheese on celery. Add raisins or peanuts for the keys on the flutes.

• Attend a local band concert.

• If your school has a band program, invite the school band to give your class a mini concert or have the band teacher talk about working with the band.

Night of the BIG CONCERT

Name:

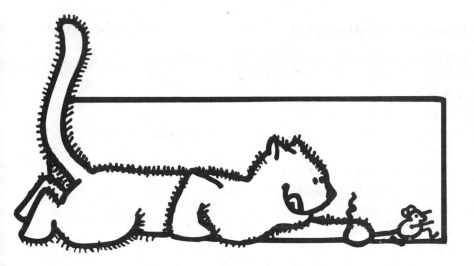

Feline Festival Day

November 7

Setting the Stage

• Under the caption: "The Cat's Out of the Bag," display a picturo of a cat coming out of a bag on the bulletin board. Add cat stories written by students on small lunch bags.

• Strategically place construction paper "paw prints" leading into and around the room. See pattern on page 44.

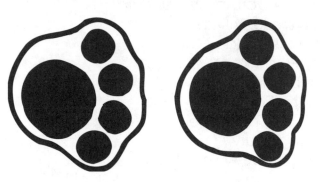

Historical Background

Belgians have been dressing up as cats and marching in parades since 1938. In the United States one of the most popular musical plays on Broadway for several years was *Cats*. Recently cats have edged out dogs as the favorite pets in America.

Literary Exploration

Anatole and the Cat by Eve Titus
The Blue Cat of Castle Town by Catherine Coblentz
Cat and Canary by Michael Foreman
The Cat Book by Kathleen Daly
Cat in the Hat by Dr. Suess
The Cat Next Door by Elizabeth Koda-Callan
Cats Are Cats by Nancy Larrick
The Cat's Burglar by Peggy Parish
Cats' Eyes by Anthony Taber

Literary Exploration continued

The Cat's Midsummer Jamboree by David Kherdian, et al
The Cat's Surprise by Marthe Seguin-Fontes
The Cat Who Went to Heaven by Elizabeth Coatsworth
Cross-Country Cat by Mary Calhoun
Duncan & Dolores (by) Barbara Samuels: A Hands-On Activity Guide by Stella Sands
The Farmyard Cat by Christine Anello
The Fat Cat: A Danish Folktale by Jack Kent
The Fire Cat by Esther Averill
Garfield (series) by Jim Davis
Great Cat by David McPhail
The Great Cat Chase by Mercer Mayer
Harry Kitten and Tucker Mouse by George Seldon
Have You Seen My Cat? by Eric Carle
Here Comes the Cat! by Vladimir Vagin and Frank Asch
It's Like This, Cat by Emily Neville
Just Cats by John Burningham
The Kid's Cat Book by Tomie de Paola
Kitten for a Day by Ezra Jack Keats
A Kitten Is Born by Heiderose Fischer-Nagel
Kitty's New Doll by Dorothy N. Kunhardt
The Little Kitten by Judy Dunn
Millions of Cats by Wanda Gag
Moon Tiger by Phyllis Root
Nobody's Cat by Miska Miles
One-Eyed Cat by Paula Fox
Puss and Boots by Charles Perrault
Socks by Beverly Cleary
Stories to Tell a Cat by Alvin Schwartz
The Tenth Good Thing About Barney by Judith Viorst
William's Ninth Life by Minna Jung
Wonderful Alexander and the Catwings by Ursula K. Le Guin

Language Experience

- Let students write about times when the "cat got their tongue" (or they got tongue-tied and were so embarrassed they did not know what to say).

- Play a new version of the "hangman" game with spelling words. Draw a cat and add four whiskers on each side for wrong letters.

Feline Festival

Feline Festival

Feline Festival

Writing Experience

• Brainstorm questions your students may have about cats. Let them write letters to the American Feline Society to get answers.

American Feline Society
204 W. 20ᵗʰ St.
New York, NY 10111

• Let students write stories entitled, "Why I Am the Cat's Meow!"

• Have students write about a day in the life of a cat or life from a cat's point of view. See reproducible on page 45.

Math Experience

⚠ Purchase fish crackers and let students do addition and subtraction problems with them. After their work has been checked, they can be the "cat" and eat the fish crackers.

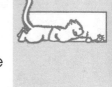

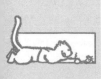

Social Studies Experience
• Discuss proper care of pets, cats in particular.

Music/Dramatic Experience
• Have students act out "The Three Little Kittens" nursery rhyme for younger students. Use the cat mask pattern on page 46.

• Check out cat songs such as: "Love for Two Cats" by Ravel, "The Cat" by B. Brittan, "Puss in Boots" by Tchaikovsky and "The Cat's Fugue" by Scarlatti from the local library.

• Sing the song, "The Old Grey Cat" as students act out the parts of cat and mice "creeping" and "sleeping."

• Read the opening chapter of *Socks*, written by Beverly Cleary. Then let students give short speeches on the merits of purchasing a new kitten for their family.

Physical/Sensory Experience

⚠ Make "paw-print" cookies using your favorite sugar cookie recipe. As the cookies come out of the oven and are quite "impressionable," use your finger to make paw prints on them.

- Use the cat face pattern on page 47 cutting out the mouth. Hang it over a doorway with string and let students throw cotton balls in the cat's mouth as they spell words. They score a point every time they spell a word correctly.

Arts/Crafts Experience

- Make cardboard cats with pipe cleaner whiskers and wiggly eyes.

- Make cat ears to wear. Cut out cat ear shapes, then fold them and staple to a headband.

Extension Activities

- Have a "Cat Show and Tell" or "Feline Festival." Let students bring their cats from home.

- Visit a local pet shop.

- Invite someone from a local animal shelter to talk about how to make a good home for a cat.

- Share miniature-size Kit-Kat™ bars for a fun treat.

44

Cut Out

Cut Out

Cut Out

Rocks and Roll Day

November 8

Setting the Stage

- Check in the school library or science room for a rock or mineral collection. Display all different kinds of rocks (all shapes, sizes, textures and colors). Encourage students to touch them and study them under a microscope or magnifying glass for a closer look. Provide an area where they can do simple tests such as scratch tests for hardness and acidity (using vinegar to see if it bubbles for the presence of limestone).

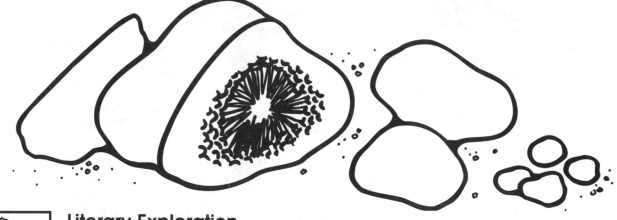

Literary Exploration

Alexandra the Rock Eater by Dorothy Van Woerkom
Everybody Needs a Rock by Byrd Baylor
The Magic School Bus Inside the Earth by Joanna Cole, et al
Smithsonian Handbooks: Rocks and Minerals by Chris Pellant
Rocks in My Pocket by Marc Harshman, et al
Stone Soup by Marcia Brown
Sylvester and the Magic Pebble by William Steig
"There Are Rocks in My Socks!" Said the Ox to the Fox by Patricia Thomas

Language Experience

- Read the story, *Stone Soup,* by Marcia Brown. See if students can tell the story with the correct sequence of events.

Writing Experience

- After reading *Sylvester and the Magic Pebble*, let students write about their adventures as rocks! See reproducible on page 52.

Math Experience

- Have students do addition and subtraction problems with small rocks or pebbles as math manipulatives. (Example: Matthew had 6 round stones but lost 2. How many does he have left?)

Science/Health Experience

- Study rocks and try to classify them.

- Make a homemade volcano. Form wet sand into the shape of a volcano with the center cored out. Put baking soda in the center, then pour vinegar into the hole on top. Look out for the lava! Another way to show how a volcano erupts is to put your thumb over a bottle of soda and shake it up a little. Let the kids watch as the pressure from inside forces the soda pop up through the top! (It's best to do this over a sink or outside.)

- Have students go on a nature walk and begin individual rock collections. They can glue their rocks in egg cartons or shoe boxes. Have them identify which rocks are igneous, sedimentary or metamorphic.

My adventures as a ROCK

Name:

Rocks and Roll Day

Rocks and Roll Day

Rocks and Roll Day

Rocks
and Roll
Day

Rocks
and Roll
Day

Rocks
and Roll
Day

Music/Dramatic Experience

• Play "rock" and roll music!

⚠ Act out the story of *Stone Soup* (asking each student to bring an item for the soup). The smell of the stone soup simmering in the crock-pot throughout the day will make them eager to eat it when it's ready.

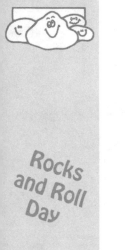

Physical/Sensory Experience

• Divide students into groups and have them categorize rocks according to color, size, shape and texture.

• Let students play the game, Rock, Paper, Scissors in pairs. A fist stands for rock; an outstretched hand is paper and two fingers criss-crossed designate scissors. Students chant, "Rock, paper, scissors," then hold out their hands in one of the symbols. Only one can be a winner unless they both come up with the same symbol. Rules: Rock crushes scissors, paper covers rock and scissors cut paper.

Arts/Crafts Experience

• Make "rock people" by painting features on smooth, clean rocks.

• Rock designs can be made by painting smooth, clean stones with two coats of poster paint. Paint designs, let them dry, then spray them with a fixative spray or paint them with clear nail polish for a glossy finish. Fine-point, fiber-tip pens can be used for adding details.

Extension Activities

- Make edible soil. Bake a pan of brownies (subsoil) with a graham cracker base (bedrock). Add frosting or chocolate pudding (topsoil).

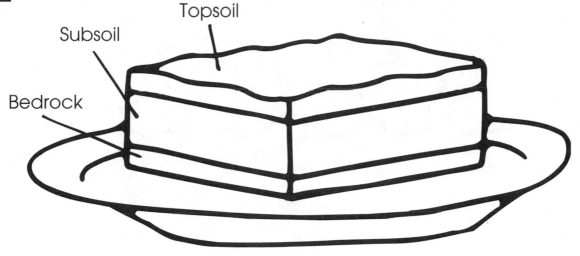

Topsoil

Subsoil

Bedrock

- Let students see the layers that form rock by adding layer upon layer of gelatin (of different colors). Add fruit or nuts for fossils!

⚠ Press cereal pieces into icing. When you lift the cereal, you'll leave behind an impression. This is a fun way to show how plants and animals leave their fossil impressions in rock layers.

- Go on a rock hunt!

- Invite a local geologist or gem cutter to talk about his or her work.

- Visit a gem and mineral show at a nearby city.

My adventures as a ROCK

Name:

Smokey Bear Day

November 9

Setting the Stage

• Set out fire prevention books or posters.

• Display a Smokey Bear stuffed animal.

• Try to borrow a firefighter's helmet to wear throughout the day.

• Make construction paper bear tracks leading into your room.

Historical Background

A bear cub survived the Lincoln National Forest fire and was found clinging to a tree. The U.S. Forest Service adopted him in cartoon form as their mascot, using him as a symbol to encourage others to avoid forest fires. Although forest fires are a natural part of the ecological process to rejuvenate new growth in the forest, many fires are caused by neglect and carelessness. Smokey Bear died on this day in 1976 at the age of 26.

Literary Exploration

Bears in the Forest by Karen Wallace
Blaze and the Forest Fire by Christopher Lampton
Deep in the Forest by Brinton Turkle
The First Forest by John Gile
Forest Fire by Patty Wolcott
A Forest Is Reborn by James Newton
Forest of Dreams by Rosemary Wells
In the Forest by Marie Hall Ets
Let's Go to Fight a Forest Fire by Michael Chester
Look at the Forest Animals by June Behrens
The Picture World of Fire Engines by Norman Barrett
Secret of the Forest by Neil Morris
Smokey Bear and the Great Wilderness by Elliott Speer Barker
Where the Forest Meets the Sea by Jeannie Baker
Who Lives in the Forest? by Diane Hearn
Woodpecker Forest by Keizaburo Tejima

Language Experience
- Discuss the pros and cons of forest fires (damage and potential harm to animals and rare plant life versus ecological cycle/process). Divide into groups to debate the issue for and against.

Writing Experience
- Write letters to Smokey Bear at our nation's capital to become Junior Forest Rangers. See reproducible on page 56.

  Smokey Bear
  Washington, D.C. 20252

- Have students use their imagination and write about how they each became an endangered species.

Science/Health Experience
- Learn about fire prevention skills.

- Brainstorm uses for wood (paper, furniture, etc.).

- Study various kinds of forest animals.

Music/Dramatic Experience
- Sing "Smokey the Bear," written by Steve Nelson and Jack Rollins.

Physical/Sensory Experience

• Conduct a mock fire drill in your room.

• Play the Old-Time Water Brigade. Divide students and have them stand in two or more parallel lines. Give each one a cup. The first team player gets water in the cup. At the signal "Go!," each team passes the water from cup to cup until they get to the end of a line where the last player pours the final cup into a bucket. The team that finishes first with the most water in their bucket is the winning team!

Arts/Crafts Experience

• Let students make posters urging people to prevent forest fires.

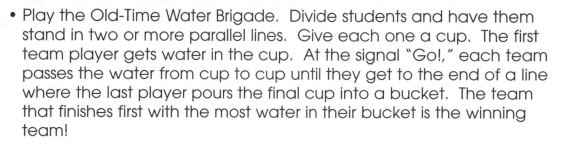

• Make Fire Marshal badges. Have each student write a sentence on the badge about how he or she will personally prevent forest fires. (Example: I will never play with matches!). See patterns on page 57.

• Have students draw a mural of the forest with trees and woodland creatures.

Extension Activities

• Contact the local fire department and arrange a class tour. Invite a firefighter to come and talk to your class.

• Make trail mix with nuts, seeds and raisins to munch on during hikes in the forest (or school yard).

• Try "Fireman Fizz" (lemon-lime soda pop) or if students are "hungry as a bear," serve "bear claws" for a treat.

Follow-Up/Homework Idea

• Have students conduct fire prevention and safety checks at home. They should look for things such as flammable materials near a combustible flame or overloaded outlets.

56

Math Madness Day

November 10

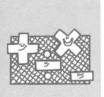
Setting the Stage

- Have students draw pictures of raised hands, writing their name on the arms. Display them on a bulletin board with the caption: "Who Loves Math?"

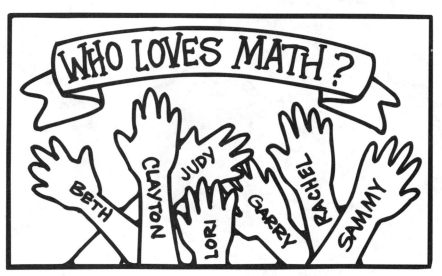

- Display math manipulatives: Unifix cubes, cuisinaire rods, parquetry blocks, dominoes or geo-boards. Children often to learn faster (with longer retention) when they have hands-on manipulatives to help them work from concrete to abstract math problems.

Literary Exploration

1,2,3 to the Zoo by Eric Carle
26 Letters and 99 Cents by Tana Hoban
Angles Are Easy as Pie by Robert Froman
Anno's Math Games by Mitsumasa Anno
Anno's Mysterious Multiplying Jar by Mitsumasa Anno
Annos Counting House by Mitsumasa Anno
The Ants Go Marching by Mary Luders
Bunches and Bunches of Bunnies by Louise Mathews
Circles by Mindel and Harry Sitomer
Circles, Triangles and Squares by Tana Hoban

Literary Exploration continued

Count and See by Tana Hoban
Dancing in the Moon: Counting Rhymes by Fritz Eichenberg
Each Orange Had 8 Slices by Paul Giganti Jr.
Eenie Meenie Miney Math! by Linda Allison and Martha Weston
Estimation by Charles Linn
Fish Eyes: A Book You Can Count On by Lois Ehlert
Gator Pie by Louise Mathews
How Big Is a Foot? by Rolf Myller
How Many Snails?: A Counting Book by Paul Giganti Jr.
How to Turn Lemons into Money by Louise Armstrong
The Icky Bug Counting Book by Jerry Pallotta
Listen to a Shape by Marcia Brown
Mathematical Games for One or Two by Mannis Charosh
Moja Means One: Swahili Counting Book by Muriel Feelings
My Animal Counting Book by Rene Cloke
Numbears by Kathleen Hague
Number Art by Leonard Everett Fisher
Number Ideas Through Pictures by Mannis Charosh
One Hungry Monster by Susan Heyboer O'Keefe
The Orange Book by Richard McGuire
Pink Pigs Aplenty by Sandy Nightingale
The Right Number of Elephants by Jeff Sheppard
Spaces, Shapes and Sizes by Jane Jonas Srivastava
Ten Little Rabbits by Virginia Grossman and Sylvia Long
Ten, Nine, Eight by Molly Bang
Time for Clocks by Daphne Harwood Trivett
Walt Disney's: 101 Dalmatians: A Counting Book by Fran Manushkin
Weighing and Balancing by Jane Jonas Srivastava

Writing Experience

- After reading, *Ten, Nine, Eight* by Molly Bang, let students pair up to write two consecutive rhyming pages in a class rhyming book. (Example: The Bear family all sat down to dine, when they realized instead of eight, there were nine. They pretended not to notice him but then, he ate more than if there had been 10.) When the book is completed, let your students read it to a kindergarten class.

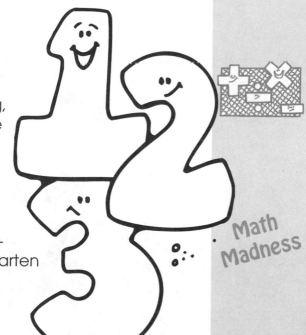

Math
Madness

Math
Madness

Math
Madness

Math Experience

⚠ Try graphing with colored cereal pieces.

• Help students learn about money by reading menu items or shopping from catalogs.

⚠ Encourage math fun: subtract round cereal "o's" (space-ships) that travel into the Black Hole (mouth).

• Teach inequalities with a hungry piranha fish (inequality symbol) that eats the biggest meal (jaws pointing towards the bigger number). Which is a snack and which is the meal?

• Teach missing addends by explaining that a puppy took a bite (or bites) out of the paper and left empty spaces. What number is missing?

• Reinforce place value with students (girls can be the tens column, boys can be the ones column). (Example, ask what 3 girls and 7 boys are in place value. Line up students to show 37.)

• Play Concentration with math problems on one set of cards and answers on the other set. Students match problems and answers. See page 63 for patterns.

Science/Health Experience

• Invite a scientist or health professional to visit your class and talk about the importance of math in various professions and how math is a part of real-life problem solving.

Social Studies Experience

• Play Math Around the World. The leader gives a problem. Students stand behind other students' desks. When the problem is called out, the first one to answer out loud gets to move to the next desk. The student who responds less quickly stays at the desk. Students can move from desk to desk around the room.

Music/Dramatic Experience

• Play "Musical Math" by leaving a drill problem on a sheet of paper on students' desks and turning on the music. Somewhat like Musical Chairs (when the music stops), the student at that desk, solves that particular problem and then writes a new one for the next student who stops there and so on.

• Sing "Learning Math Is Fun to Do" (to the tune of "Mary Had a Little Lamb").

> Learning math is fun to do,
> Fun to do,
> Fun to do.
> Learning math is fun to do;
> We use it every day!

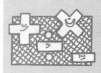

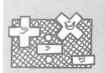

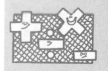
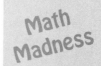

Math Madness

Math Madness

Math Madness

Physical/Sensory Experience

⚠ Add spice to student responses by letting them write their answers in the palm of their hands, on a small chalkboard, with Cheez Whiz™ on a cracker or finger the number on top of a zip-type bag filled with pudding.

• Give students various manipulatives to work with, finding new combinations of answers. (Example: The answer is 7. What is the question? 2 + 5, 15 - 8, 7 x 1, etc.)

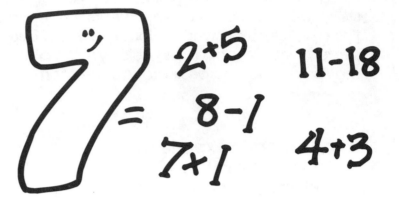

Extension Activities

⚠ Play Math Bingo. Give each student a Bingo card that they can fill with answers from possibilities you list on the board. As you give math problems, they cover their answers with Skittles™ or m & m's™ or small treats. See reproducibles on page 64.

⚠ When students need a little "pick-me-up," Math Munchies (a nutritious snack such as raisins) can enhance mathematical analysis and computational skills! And they sure taste good!

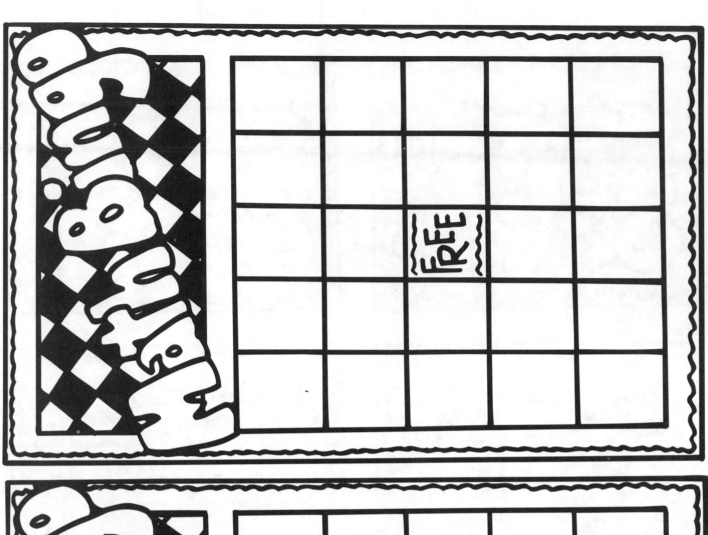

Veterans Day

November 11
(varies)

Setting the Stage
- Display American flags and patriotic symbols. Army surplus stores sometimes have excess military items to donate to a worthy cause, or ask neighbors for old army boots that could be displayed.

Historical Background
On this day, an armistice was signed ending World War I in 1918. Originally called Armistice Day, it was later changed to Veterans Day to honor all soldiers. Honoring the Tomb of the Unknowns in Arlington National Cemetery began on this day in 1921. Today we honor all those who have served in our country's armed forces.

Literary Exploration
My Daddy Was a Soldier: A World War II Story by Deborah Kogan Ray
Veteran's Day by Lynda Sorenson
Waiting for the Evening Star by Rosemary Wells
The Wall by Eve Bunting
A Wall of Names by Judy Donnelly
What Is Veteran's Day? by Margot Parker

Language Experience
- Discuss what it would be like to defend your country in time of war or to be a civilian in a country torn apart by war.

- Discuss the Tomb of the Unknowns monument in Arlington National Cemetery.

Writing Experience
• Write a letter to the "Unknown Soldier" or to a veteran, expressing thanks for fighting for America's freedom. See reproducible on page 68.

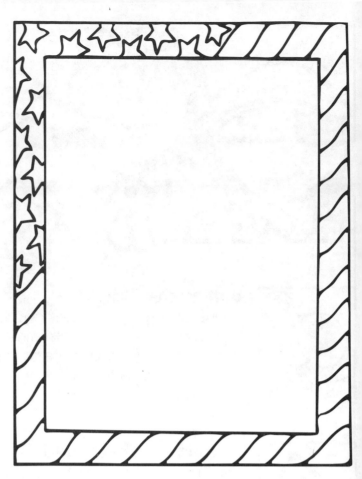

Social Studies Experience
• Conduct a brief discussion about the history of war and conflict. Explain why countries have able-bodied men and women go to war to defend them.

• Invite someone who has served in the U.S. Air Force, Navy, Army or Marines to come and speak to the class.

• Invite a native of a country where war has been a firsthand experience to talk to the class.

Music/Dramatic Experience
- Observe two minutes of silence at 11:00 a.m. Great Britain was the first to observe two minutes of silence in 1919 to honor those who died in World War I.

Physical/Sensory Experience
- Let students pretend they are marching in a Veterans Day parade.

Arts/Crafts Experience
- Help students make army hats. Find a bowl big enough to fit a child's head. Use it as a mold, and papier-mâché around it. Let it dry, then remove the bowl. Trim the hat and paint it.

- Let students create banners to place on the doors of their houses to honor veterans. Burlap or felt can be used on a wooden dowel.

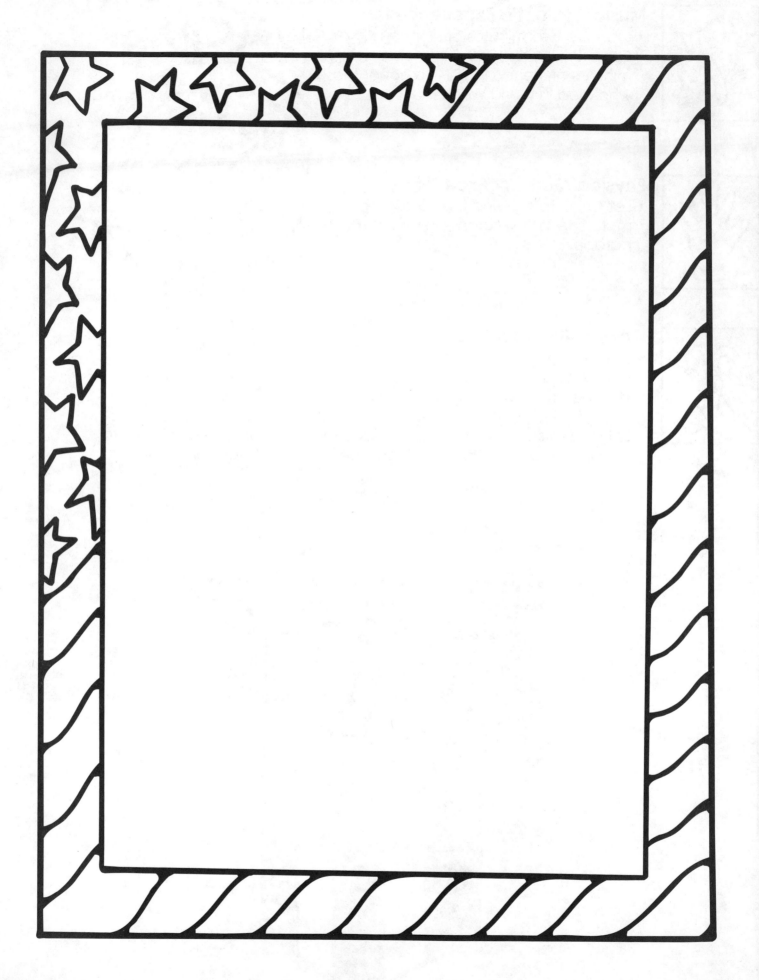

68

Dollars and Sense Day

November 12

Setting the Stage
• Let students start "earning" coins through good behavior or completed work to redeem at a class store to purchase items.

Historical Background
Discuss the history of our exchange system. Money is our current system of exchange for goods and services. Prior to the use of coins and currency, people used everything from salt and beads to grains and cloth. How would your students like to buy a new pair of shoes with a couple of dried fish? Coins originated around 600 B.C. and paper money was probably introduced by the Chinese in the early 1200s.

Literary Exploration
Alexander, Who Used to Be Rich Last Sunday by Judith Viorst
Arthur's Funny Money by Lillian Hoban
Dollars and Cents for Harriet by Betsy Maestro
Elephant Eats the Profits by Jacquelyn Reinach
The Fisherman Who Needed a Knife: A Story About Why People Use Money by Marie Winn
How Much Is a Million? by David Schwartz
How to Turn Lemons into Money by Louise Armstrong
If You Made a Million by David M. Schwartz
Matthew and the Midnight Money Van by Allen Morgan
"Smart" a poem from *Where the Sidewalk Ends* by Shel Silverstein

Language Experience

• Discuss the uses and importance of an exchange system.

• Play the Wordsworth Game. Assign every letter of the alphabet a monetary value (Example: A = 1 cent, B = 2 cents). Then have students figure out how much their names are worth, or have them write a complete sentence under $1.00.

Writing Experience

• Have students write about what they would do if they had a million dollars. See reproducible on page 72.

• Have students write about what they would do if there were no money.

• Ask students to write about what they would do if money grew on trees.

• Have students write to their parents stating a case for why they deserve more allowance than what they are presently getting.

• See reproducible for writing activities on page 73.

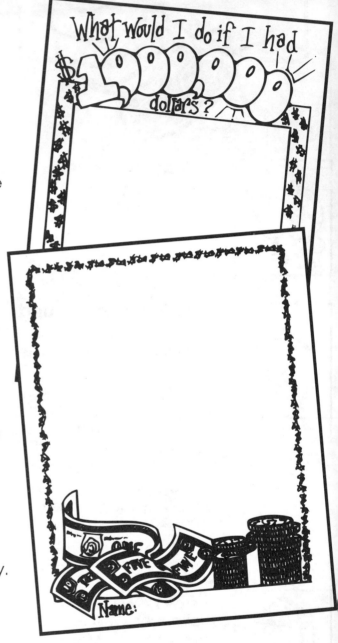

What would I do if I had $1,000,000 dollars?

Name:

Math Experience

• Learn about the monetary value of coins and currency.

Social Studies Experience

• Discuss the symbols, designs and people depicted on various coins and currency and how they portray American history and culture.

• Bring coins from various countries and teach students their names and monetary values.

70

Music/Dramatic Experience

- Set up a classroom store. Display empty food boxes with price tags on them. Invite students to take turns being the cashier, sales clerk or shoppers in the store, practicing buying items and counting change.

Physical/Sensory Experience

- Have a penny-pitching contest. Pitch pennies against a wall to see whose lands closest to a target.

Arts/Crafts Experience

- Make coin rubbings. Put a coin under paper and rub it with the side of the pencil until the coin's design is revealed.

Extension Activities

- Invite a coin collector to display his or her collection and talk about it to your class. Challenge students to begin coin collections of their own.

⚠ Foil-covered chocolate coins can be purchased in most stores and will add a little fun to the day!

- Invite a banker to come and talk about his work, or take students to visit a bank.

Values Education Experience

- Teach the importance of budgeting money.

Follow-Up/Homework Idea

- Give students a problem to take home: If your parents gave you $10.00 to spend at the grocery store, what could you buy to provide dinner for two people?

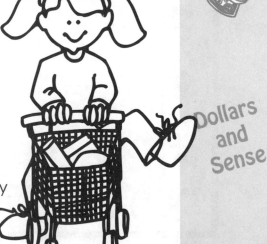

What would I do if I had 1,000,000 dollars?

Name:

Name:

Wampum
Day

Wampum
Day

Wampum
Day

Wampum Day

November 13

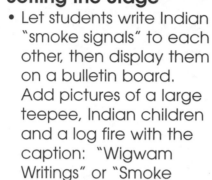

Setting the Stage

• Let students write Indian "smoke signals" to each other, then display them on a bulletin board. Add pictures of a large teepee, Indian children and a log fire with the caption: "Wigwam Writings" or "Smoke Signals." See reproducible on page 81.

• Make a full-sized Native American costume out of paper or fabric and attach it to a full-length mirror. Students can stand in front of the mirror and imagine how they might have looked back in early America.

• Have students draw or paint a mural scene including land, water, canoes and teepees or wigwams.

Historical Background

When early settlers came to the "New World," people were already living here. When Columbus had arrived earlier, he thought he had discovered the Indies so he called the people "Indians." As we celebrate our country's first Thanksgiving, we remember that the "Indian" peoples are an important part of our American heritage.

74

Literary Exploration

Counting Rhyme: Ten Little Indians by Tadasu Izawa
Dancing with the Indians by Angela Medearis
The Games Indians Played by Sigmund Lavine
How Indians Really Lived by Gordon Curtis Baldwin
I Can Read About Indians by Elizabeth Warren
Indian Children of America by Margaret Farquhar
Indian in the Cupboard by Lynne Reid Banks
Let's Be Indians by Peggy Parish
Morning Girl by Michael Dorris
Return of the Indian by Lynne Reid Banks
Squanto by Feenie Ziner
Squanto, Friend of the Pilgrims by Clyde Robert Bulla
Squanto: The Indian Who Saved the Pilgrims by James Rothaus, et al
Squanto: The Pilgrim Adventure by Kate Jassem
The Story of Pocahontas, Indian Princess by Patricia Adams

Writing Experience

- Have students write about what a totem pole might say if it could talk. See reproducible on page 82.

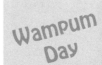

Writing Experience continued

- Have students write letters using Native American symbols for authentic-looking leather paintings. Soak brown paper bags in water, then unfold them. Carefully squeeze out the excess water, then smooth the paper and iron it flat with a warm iron. This gives it a "leathery" look and feel. After it is dry, students may write with colored markers or paint Native American symbols to make messages. Some may want to cut around the edges of the paper to resemble an animal hide. See page 83 for symbols.

- Have students write about their adventures as Native Americans that first Thanksgiving.

Math Experience

- Illustrate adding three or more addends with "Totem Pole Math." Add each piece of the totem pole (and number) at a time.

Social Studies Experience

- The Native American cultures are richly diverse in their history, customs and territory. Research some of the regional differences such as: housing, clothing, transportation, food, trade, etc.

Music/Dramatic Experience

- Set up a teepee in the room and let students dress up as Native Americans and role-play.

- Sing "Go My Son" written by Burson-Nofchissey.

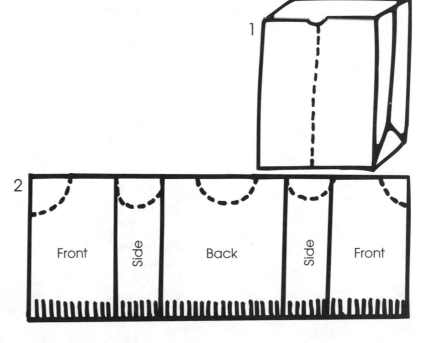

Physical/Sensory Experience

- Let students make up tribal "rain" dances and perform them.

Arts/Crafts Experience

- Make Indian vests from large, paper grocery sacks. Scrunch the bag into a small ball and wet it entirely. Iron it dry. Cut off the bottom of the sack and cut up the front (center) of one of the wide sides. Spread the sack out and cut it as shown. Cut a fringe around the bottom. Tape at shoulders.

1

2

| Front | Side | Back | Side | Front |

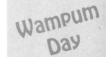

Wampum Day

Wampum Day

Wampum Day

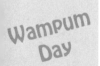

Arts/Crafts Experience continued

- Have students make beaded necklaces. Color macaroni with food coloring and let it dry on wax paper. String the macaroni on long pieces of yarn and tie them around their necks.

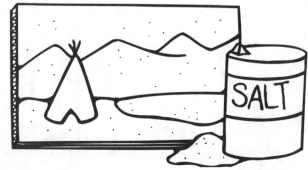

- Let students work together to make an Indian totem pole out of toilet paper tubes or thread spools, then paint it.

- Indian necklaces can be made from paper coffee filters. Cut the center out of a smooth coffee filter, then cut small slits around the outer edge. Students paint with a food coloring/water mixture, watercolors or colored markers, making Native American symbols or designs along the fluted edge. Cut a slit in one end to fit it around the neck. Students may punch two holes in it and thread yarn through to wear around the neck.

- Show students how to make salt-dough beads for necklaces. Poke a needle through the hole to make an opening before it hardens, then it will be easy to put the yarn through the beads after they are painted.

- Students can make clay pottery by coiling bits of clay into ring shapes and layering each ring on top of the other.

- Let students try their hands at Navajo sand paintings. Use sand (or salt) mixed with dry tempera paint on a cardboard background. Mix equal parts of glue and water and apply the mixture to the cardboard on any sketched design. Sprinkle the sand or salt mixture onto the cardboard. It will adhere to the background. Shake off the excess.

Arts/Crafts Experience

• Let students design Indian canoes out of construction paper. Cut out paper canoe shapes, then punch holes along the sides. Students can thread brown yarn through the holes. Let them also make an Indian brave or squaw sitting in the canoe.

• Students can make Native American accessories from construction paper and a little imagination! For chain necklaces, interlock colored 1' x 6" strips; for headbands fit a long strip around the head and decorative paper "feathers." For arrows, cut paper triangular shapes and fasten them to the ends of straws. Necklaces can be made out of colored noodles or cereal. See headband pattern on page 84.

• Sand patterns can be made into beautiful designs much like Native American sand paintings. Mix salt or sand and dry tempera paint, layering different colors in a clear jar. Warn students not to shake or mix the layered colors together. After all the layers have been made, have students stick a pencil or pointed object down the sides of the jar to create an interesting edge "bleeding" the colors.

• Moccasins can be made from old socks. Cut off the tops, then sew a 1/4" hem along the edge to make a casing for a yarn drawstring. Students can glue on beads, small bells or colored macaroni for added decoration.

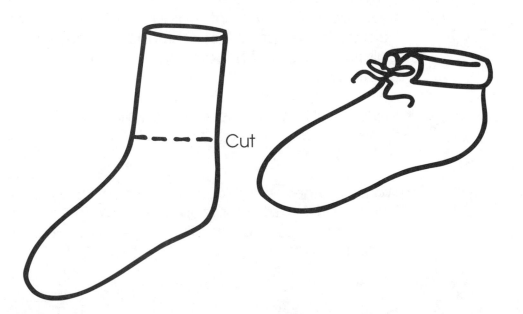

Cut

Extension Activities

⚠ Make a fruit totem pole by decorating different kinds of citrus fruits with colored markers. Skewer them on a dowel with the biggest fruit on the bottom and the smallest at the top.

⚠ Make Indian Hoe-Cake by mixing: 1 cup cornmeal, 1 tsp. salt, 3 T. butter and 3/4 cup boiling water. Quickly pour the mixture onto a greased cookie sheet and spread it evenly. Bake at 300°F for 45 minutes. Cut it into three dozen pieces of cake. Students can make homemade butter by putting a half a pint of whipping cream in a clear jar and shaking it until it is solid.

⚠ Show students how to make an edible teepee from half a flour tortilla. Form the tortilla half into a cone shape with a little opening at the top. Use several straight toothpicks dipped into frosting as a frame to hold up the teepee. Decorate the outside of the tortilla teepee by painting designs with food coloring and water. Pretzels can serve as paintbrushes.

• Invite local Native Americans to visit your class and share their heritage (dancing; making fry bread; showing clay pottery, silver or native artifacts).

• Work together on a model of a Native American village. Place sugar cones upside down for teepees. Trees can be made from toilet paper tubes and construction paper. Let students be creative to see what they can come up with on their own!

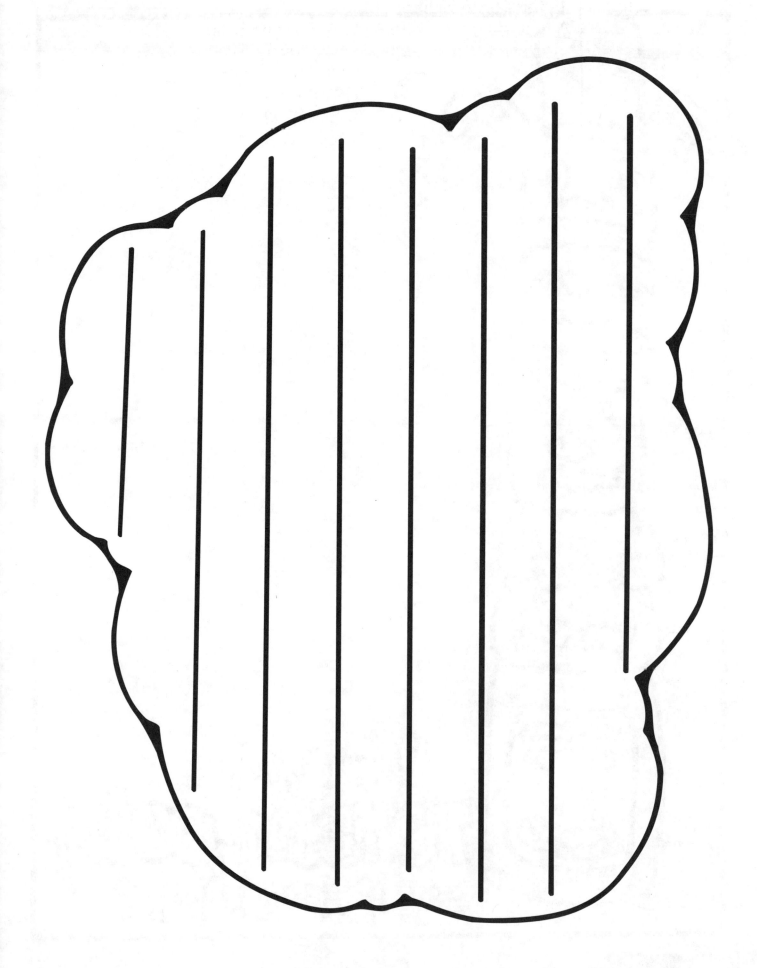

What would a totem pole say if it could talk?

Name:

Native American Symbols

Water	Snake	Moon	Sun	Peace Pipe
Teepee	Rainbow	Rain Cloud	Happiness	
Swift	Pony Tracks	Mountain	Hunt	
Fish	Star	Horse	Protection	
All	Friendship	Deer	Bear	Woman
Man	Buffalo	Rain	Wise	Grain

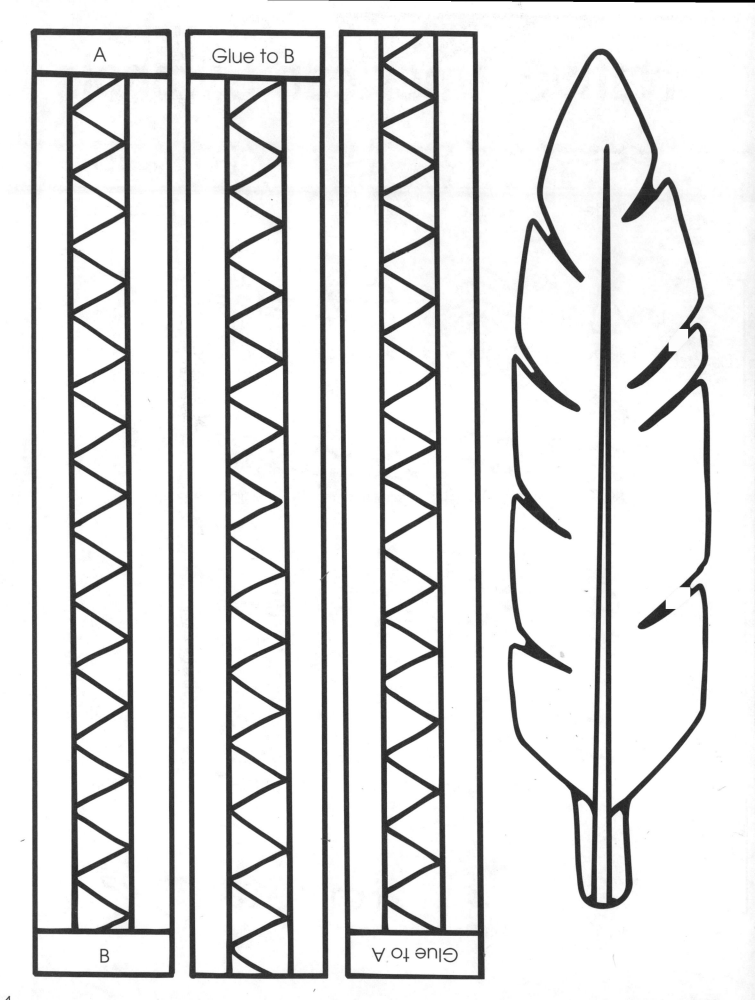

A

Glue to B

B

Glue to B

Glue to A

84

Claude Monet's Birthday

November 14

Setting the Stage
• Display various books about Monet and some of his art prints.

Historical Background
Claude Monet was an important French painter born on this day in 1840.

 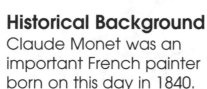

Literary Exploration
Blue Butterfly: A Story About Claude Monet by Bijou Le Tord
Claude Monet by Ann Waldron
The Magical Garden of Claude Monet by Laurence Anholt

Language Experience
• Many artists such as Monet were never given the credit they deserved for their work while they were alive. Have a discussion about whether critics can have an effect on a person's work.

Writing Experience

• Have students write about how they might convince others of the aesthetic value of the work they do.

Science/Health Experience

• Monet would often paint the same subject at different times throughout the day to note its subtle changes. Study the effects of light on objects at different times today.

Social Studies Experience

• Study art history up to the movement called "Impressionism" which was inspired by Monet's painting, Impressionism: *Sunrise*.

• Study the life of this French painter.

Music/Dramatic Experience

- Let students paint while you play music of Monet's era (such as Claude Debussy's).

Arts/Crafts Experience

- Let students try their hand at "Impressionism." Let them concentrate on different angles, lighting and time of day with their painting.

Extension Activities

- Students will enjoy doing their own "impressionism" in pudding paintings (pudding on wax paper).

- Schedule a field trip to a local art exhibit that includes Monet's work.

Children's Book Day

November 15

Setting the Stage

- Display a variety of children's books around the room to create excitement and interest!

- Create a bulletin board with giant paper flowers. Inside each flower display a book jacket. Add this caption: "Take Your Pick!"

- Begin a bulletin board that will also serve as a reading tracking system. Decorate an area to look like library shelves. Place different sizes and colors of construction paper strips to look like books on the shelves. When a student finishes a book, he or she writes the title and author on one of the strips.

- Label an area with the caption: "Take a Giant Step in Reading." As students finish books they fill out foot shapes with the titles. The footsteps can trek all around the room. See pattern for foot on page 99.

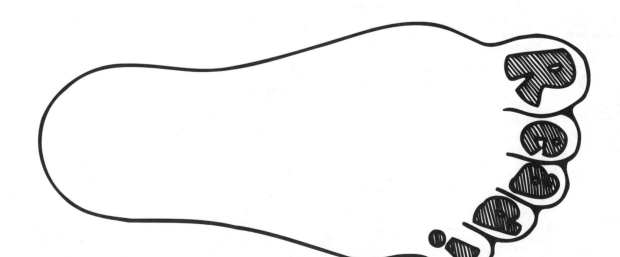

88

Setting the Stage continued

- Display a rabbit coming out of a hat with the caption: "Find the Magic in Reading!" Add paper stars around the rabbit. Write book titles on the stars or display book jackets for reading possibilities.

- Set up an island area with palm trees, coconuts, starfish and shells. Display books in a crate. Use the caption: "Books I'd Like to Take to a Desert Island!" Use a treasure chest and title it "Find Treasures in Reading!"

- Make a moon exploration or space travel board with the caption: "Start Some Exploring of Your Own with Books!"

- Start a worm or train on the wall. Let it stretch all over the room with titles of books students read. Every time a child reads or shares a book with the class, they can add another section. Add the caption: "Hey, Bookworm! Inch on over here to a good book!"

- Bring an old bathtub (with legs) to class. Let students paint it or put colored decals and stickers all over it. Fill it with pillows or stuffed animals and let kids relax and read.

Children's Book Day

Children's Book Day

Children's Book Day

- Make a bulletin board with book jackets from favorite books with the book jackets "popping" out.

- Place paper "doors" on a bulletin board. Let them open to different subjects such as: travel, fantasy, sports and heroes. Add the caption: "Reading Opens Many Doors."

Setting the Stage continued

• Draw a zoo animal in a cage. Put it on the wall with the caption: "Escape with a Good Book."

• Place pictures of football players on a bulletin board. Surround them with book jackets. Add the caption: "Try Tackling a Good Book!"

• Place a globe or world map next to books or book jackets under the caption: "Discover the Wonderful World of Books!"

• Begin a Banana Split Challenge! Encourage students to tell about books they read to earn/add ingredients to their split throughout the year. At the end of the year, have a banana split party and enjoy the "fruits" of their labor! See reproducible on page 100.

_____ can earn a

Banana Split Party!

*Every 100 pages adds to your creation

Napkin _____
Spoon _____
Bowl _____
Banana _____
Scoop _____
Topping _____
Whipped Cream _____
Cherry _____

Scoop _____
Topping _____
Whipped Cream _____
Nuts _____
Cherry _____
Scoop _____
Topping _____

Setting the Stage continued

- Challenge students to go an entire week without turning on the TV, but read instead. As a class, brainstorm a list of 20 things they can do instead of watching TV (play a board game, finish a puzzle or bake treats for neighbors, etc.).

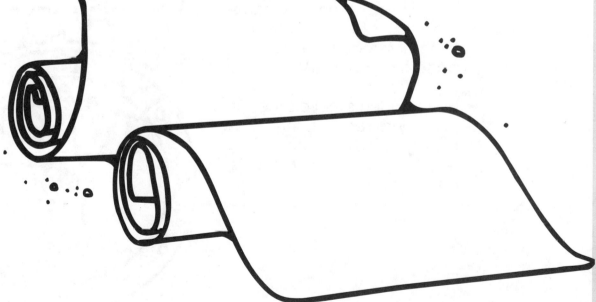

Historical Background

The first books were papyrus rolls used in Rome and Greece. These were handwritten by paid professionals or slaves. During the Middle Ages, books with pages bound together were handwritten by monks. With the invention of the printing press, the first major project was the printing of the Gutenberg Bible. Today, Children's Book Week is observed the second week in November.

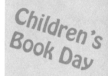

Literary Exploration

Good Books, Good Times! by Lee Bennett Hopkins
How a Book Is Made by Aliki
I Like Books by Anthony Brown
"Jimmy Jet and His TV Set" a poem from *Where the Sidewalk Ends* by
   Shel Silverstein
Little Old Man Who Couldn't Read by Irma Simonton Black
A Story, a Story by Gail Haley
Too Many Books by Caroline Feller Bauer
When Will I Read? by Lillian Hoban
You Read to Me, I'll Read to You by John Ciardi

Language Experience

• Let students bring and share their favorite books to tell about.
  Brainstorm creative types of book reporting.

• Discuss different literary genre, then let students express their particular tastes. Include picture books, fiction and non-fiction, fantasy,
  action stories, legends, fables, historical fiction, mysteries, folktales, tall
  tales, poetry, biographies, autobiographies and fairy tales.

• Set aside a daily-sustained silent
  reading time. Call it something
  fun: R.A.C.E. (read a chapter
  everyday) Time. Have students
  create a R.A.C.E. clock and pin
  it to their shirts. Have students
  attach the hands to the clock
  with a brad. Then they can set
  their clocks for a drop-every-
  thing-and-read time. See
  pattern on page 101.

• Have students fold a sheet of
  paper into sections, then draw
  pictures of what happened
  sequentially (the main events) in
  a favorite book.

R.A.C.E.
Read a Chapter Everyday
TIME:

Writing Experience

- Ask students to write about what kind of characters they would choose to be and why. See reproducible on page 102.

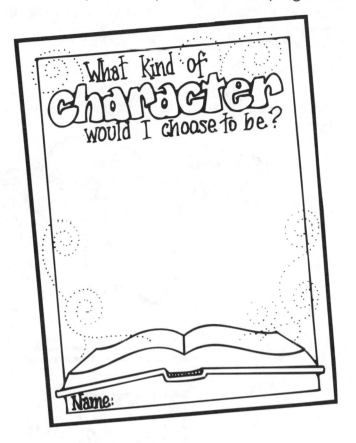

- Write a letter to one of the characters in a favorite book.

Math Experience

- Let students survey others about their favorite books. Make a graph to let students chart the results.

Social Studies Experience

- Discuss the history of books: how they were first made, how accessible they were to people, etc.

Children's Book Day

Children's Book Day

Children's Book Day

Music/Dramatic Experience

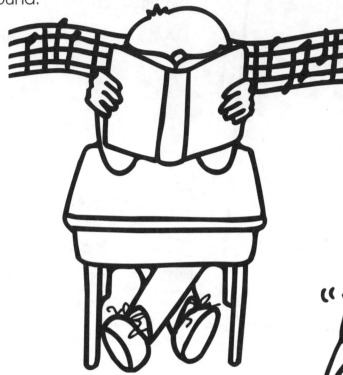

- Let students debate the merits of reading books versus watching TV.

- Divide students into groups and have them act out their favorite books.

- Encourage students to dress up as their favorite book characters.

- Allow students to read as you play soft classical music in the background.

- Have each student create a commercial to convince others to read a certain book.

Physical/Sensory Experience

- Let students sit under a tree and read in the shade!

- Discuss the use and care of books. Talk about the importance of having clean hands, keeping books safe from rain, pets or small children, and not turning pages down at the corners.

- Let students practice good posture by balancing books on their heads as they walk. Make it a competitive relay!

Arts/Crafts Experience

• Students can create personalized bookmarks. See patterns for some bookmarks on page 103.

• Let students create posters encouraging everyone to read.

• Have students design book jackets for favorite books.

• Students will enjoy creating and wearing large buttons that encourage reading.

• Let students make picture books sequencing important events in favorite books.

• Have students make shoe box dioramas from scenes in favorite books.

• Let students paint a mural together depicting scenes from a favorite book.

Extension Activities

- Take students to the public library. Ask a librarian to give a special presentation on the children's book section.

- Host a classroom or school-wide Read-a-Thon. Set desks aside and provide pillows, lawn chairs and blankets. Let students find comfortable spots anywhere around the room to "camp out" and read all afternoon.

- Invite parents, the principal, custodian or other people who play various roles in the school to read their favorite children's books to your class.

- Have a class Book Swap. Let students bring old favorites to trade.

- Implement a home-reading program, giving students an opportunity to take books home to read, obtain a parent signature, then bring back for a new book.

Values Education Experience

- Discuss the importance of reading consistently. Research shows the importance of daily reading to stimulate an interest and love of books! Reading aloud helps a student's verbal development, listening skills, increased attentive ability and socio-emotional development. It also helps students gain valuable feelings of confidence and experience as they share thoughts and feelings vicariously through books about faraway people and places! Set aside a regular quiet time each day just for reading.

Values Education Experience continued

Introduce students to books from this list:

Picture Books

All in the Woodland Early by Jane Yolen
The Amazing Bone by William Steig
The Aminal by Lorna Balian
Animals Should Definitely Not Wear Clothing by Judy Barrett
Anno's Counting Book by Mitsumasa Anno
Anno's Journey by Mitsumasa Anno
Apt. 3 by Ezra Jack Keats
Arrow to the Sun by Gerald McDermott
The Baby's Bedtime Book by Kay Chorao
Big, Bad Bruce by Bill Peet
Changes, Changes by Pat Hutchins
Close Your Eyes by Jean Marzollo
Coco Can't Wait by Taro Gomi
Curlicues, the Fortunes of Two Pug Dogs by Valerie Worth
Dandelion by Don Freeman
Dawn by Uri Schulveitz
Do You Know? by B.G. Ford
Dressing by Helen Oxenbury
Each Peach Pear Plum by Janet and Allan Ahlberg
Ed Emberley's Drawing Book of Animals by Barbara Emberley
Finger Rhymes by Marc Brown
Fireflies in the Night by Judy Hawes
The First Words Picture Book by Bill Gillham
Frederick by Leo Lionni
George and Martha by George Marshall
Geraldine's Blanket by Holly Keller
The Great Take-Away by Louise Mathews
Harry and the Terrible Whatzit by Dick Quackenbush
Hooray for Me! by Remy and Charlip
I Can-Can You? by Peggy Parish
I Met a Man by John Ciardi
The Indoor Noisy Book by Margaret Wise Brown
Look What I Can Do by Jose Aruego
Madeline by Ludwig Bemelmans
Mama's Secret by Maria Polushkin
Max's First Word by Rosemary Wells
Millions and Millions and Millions by Louis Slobodkin
My Wonder Book by R. Odor
Nailheads and Potato Eyes by Cynthia Basil
Noah's Ark by Peter Spier
Obadiah the Bold by Brinton Turkle
On Market Street by Arnold Lobel
Peter's Chair by Ezra Jack Keats
A Pocket Full of Cricket by Rebecca Caudill
Rosie's Walk by Pat Hutchins
Sam Who Never Forgets by Eve Rice
Serendipity books (series) by Stephen Cosgrove
The Shrinking of Treehorn by Florence Heide
Sleepy Book by Charlotte Zolotow
The Stonecutter by Gerald McDermott
Stopping by Woods on a Snowy Evening by Robert Frost
A Story, a Story by Gail Haley
Take Another Look by Tana Hoban
Three Billy Goats Gruff by Marcia Brown
Tikki Tikki Tembo by Arlene Mosel
The Very Nice Things by Jean Merrill

Children's Book Day

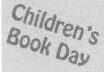

Children's Book Day

Children's Book Day

Wait for William by Marjory Flack
What Will It Be? by Jane Belk Moncure
What's That You Said? by Ann Weiss
Who Am I? by June Behrens
Will's Quill by Don Freeman
William's Doll by Charlotte Zolotow

Junior Middle Readers

Anastasia Krupnik by Lois Lowry
Bambi by Felix Salton
Black Beauty by Anna Sewell
Black Cauldron by Lloyd Alexander
Bridge to Terabithia by Katherine Paterson
Bronze Bow by Elizabeth Spears
Call It Courage by Armstrong Sperry
Call of the Wild by Jack London
The Cay by Theodore Taylor
Charlotte's Web by E.B. White
The Cricket in Times Square by George Seldon
The Door in the Wall by Mauguerite DeAngeli
The Forgotten Door by Alexander Key
From the Mixed Up Files of Mrs. Basil E. Frankweiler by Elaine Konigsberg
Gentle Ben by Walt Morey
The Girl Who Cried Flowers by Jane Yolen
The Great Brain (series) by John Fitzgerald
The Grey King by Susan Cooper
Harriet the Spy by Louise Fitzhugh
Heidi by Johanna Spyri
Homer Price by Robert McCloskey
The Incredible Journey by Sheila Burnsford
Island of the Blue Dolphins by Scott O'Dell
The Lemonade Trick by Scott Corbett
Mary Poppins by Pamela Travers
Mrs. Frisby and the Rats of Nimh by Robert O' Brien
My Side of the Mountain by Jean George
Old Yeller by Fred Gipson
The Ordinary Princess by M.M. Kaye
Owls in the Family by Farley Mowat
Pippi Longstocking by Astrid Lindgren
Pushcart War by Jean Merrill
Robinson Crusoe by Daniel Defoe
Roll of Thunder, Hear My Cry by Mildred Taylor
The Secret Garden by Frances Burnett
Shoeshine Girl by Clyde Bulla
Sing Down the Moon by Scott O'Dell
Sounder by William Armstrong
The Summer of the Swans by Betsy Bryars
A Taste of Blackberries by Doris B. Smith
Trumpet of the Swan by E. B. White
Tuck Everlasting by Natalie Babbitt
The Voyages of Doctor Doolittle by Hugh Lofting
Where the Lillies Bloom by Vera and Bill Cleaver
Where the Red Fern Grows by Wilson Rawls
Where the Sidewalk Ends by Shel Silverstein
The Wizard of Oz by Frank Baum
The Wind in the Willows by Kenneth Grahame
A Wrinkle in Time by Madeleine L'Engle
The Yearling by Marjorie Rawlings

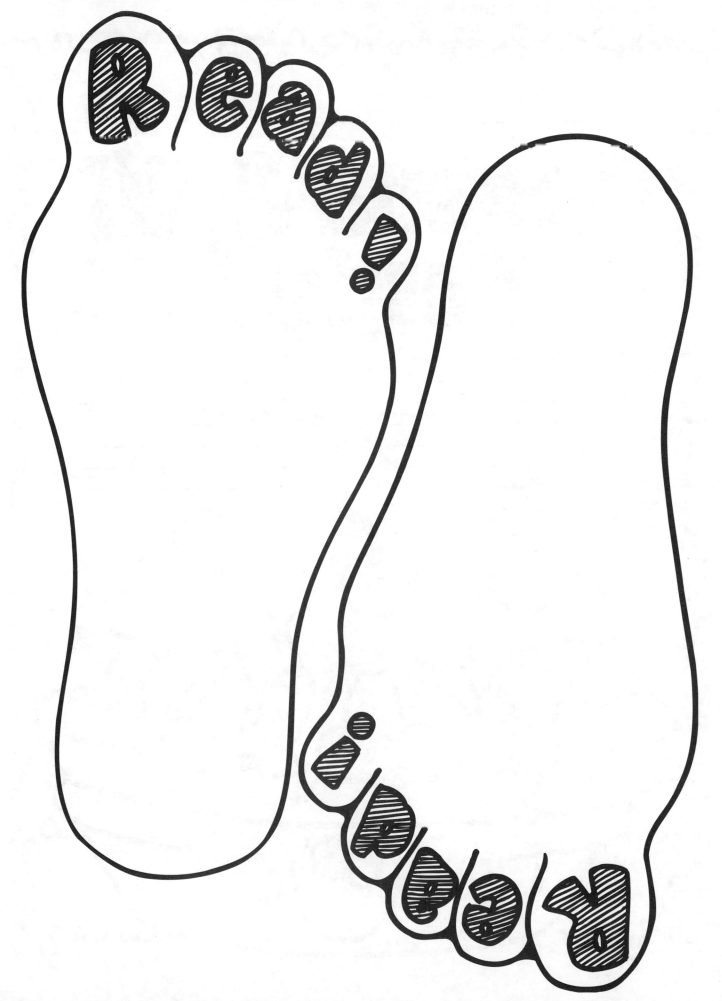

_____ can earn a

Banana Split Party!

* Every 100 pages adds to your creation

Napkin _____
Spoon _____
Bowl _____
Banana _____
Scoop _____
Topping _____
Whipped Cream _____
Cherry _____

Scoop _____
Topping _____
Whipped Cream _____
Nuts _____
Cherry _____
Scoop _____
Topping _____

What kind of **Character** would I choose to be?

Name:

Talkin' Turkey Day

November 16

Setting the Stage

- Display a large paper turkey body on a bulletin board. Fan out large construction paper feathers (on which students have written tall tales). Add the caption: "Look Who's Talkin' Turkey!" See patterns for turkey head and feet on pages 111-112. The turkey body can be a 12" circle.

- Put up samples of student work under the caption: "No Turkeys at (name of school)!"

- Make a giant paper turkey body. Have students trace their hands on colored construction paper for turkey feathers.

Setting the Stage continued

• Have students draw individualized turkeys, then "dress" them with fabric scraps. Display them with the caption: "Turkey Dressing."

• Make turkey tracks leading into the classroom or arrange them around the chalkboard. See patterns for turkey tracks on page 113.

Literary Exploration

Don't Eat Too Much Turkey! by Miriam Cohen
Sometimes It's Turkey, Sometimes It's Feathers by Lorna Balian
Turkey in the Straw by Barbara Shook Hazen
Turkey on the Loose by Sylvie Wickstrom

Language Experience

• Let students draw turkeys and write words on them with many synonym possibilities. (Examples: GIANT —huge, large, enormous, gigantic, humongous)

Writing Experience

- Have students make up recipes for turkey. Brainstorm fun ideas such as: turkey soup, turkey casserole, turkey gelatin, turkey pie, turkey ice cream or turkey omelet.

- Have students decide who gets the turkey wishbone (themselves, a teacher, another student, the President of the United States, etc.). Let them write about what that person might wish for and why.

- Let students draw and cut out turkeys, then write what they are thankful for on the feathers.

- Have each student write about an embarrassing situation with the title, "I Made a Turkey Out of Myself!"

- Let students be creative and write stories about "How to Catch a Turkey!"

- Have students write recipes from memory for how to cook a turkey.

- See reproducible for writing activities on page 114.

Name:

Science/Health Experience

• Visit a local poultry farm. Compare the size and color of a turkey egg with a chicken egg.

Music/Dramatic Experience

• Sing "Gobble, Gobble, Gobble" by Margaret L. Simpson and June M. Norton.

Physical/Sensory Experience

• Play Pin the Feather on the Turkey. Use the patterns on pages 115-116.

Talkin'
Turkey

Talkin'
Turkey

Talkin'
Turkey

Arts/Crafts Experience

• Have students trace around their hands to create turkeys.

• Let students draw turkeys on construction paper or light cardboard. Provide seeds or dried beans or squares of colored tissue paper for them to glue on the outlines.

Arts/Crafts Experience continued

- Let students make a "trotting turkey"! Copy the turkey pattern. Have them cut out the circles and poke their fingers through to make the turkey walk. See patterns on page 117.

- Have students draw a turkey face on tagboard. They can make a turkey body from a pinecone. Feathers can be made by sticking leaves in the pinecone. They will need to glue the paper face to the pinecone.

Extension Activities

- Host a classroom Turkey Trot to help students share in the joy of giving. Ask a local grocer to donate a turkey. Have students bring canned goods for needy families at a local shelter. Tell students their names will be entered in a drawing every time they donate an item. Explain that the probability of winning is increased with each Item they bring. On the day of the drawing have participating students run around the school yard. At the end of the "Turkey Trot" announce the winner of the drawing!

Extension Activities continued

⚠ Make edible turkeys that are cute and tasty! Use a round cookie or cracker for a base. Use frosting to glue a half cookie or cracker to the round base. Add a chocolate kiss "body" to the cookie base and a candy corn "head" to the body. Add candy corn pieces fanning out like turkey feathers along the half cookie back. Add a red hot under the candy corn head for the turkey wattle! It will look almost too good to eat!

⚠ Stick construction paper feathers and a paper head into the back-side of an apple with toothpicks. Add craft stick legs and gumdrop feet for a fun turkey.

• Host an annual Turkey Bowl (flag football) game outside.

• Have kids "stuff the turkey" (trash can) with trash from the day's activities.

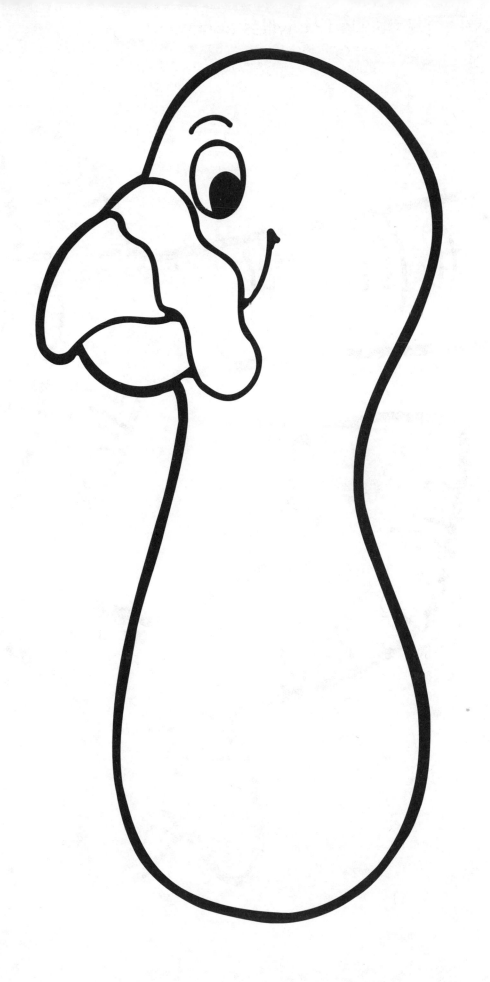

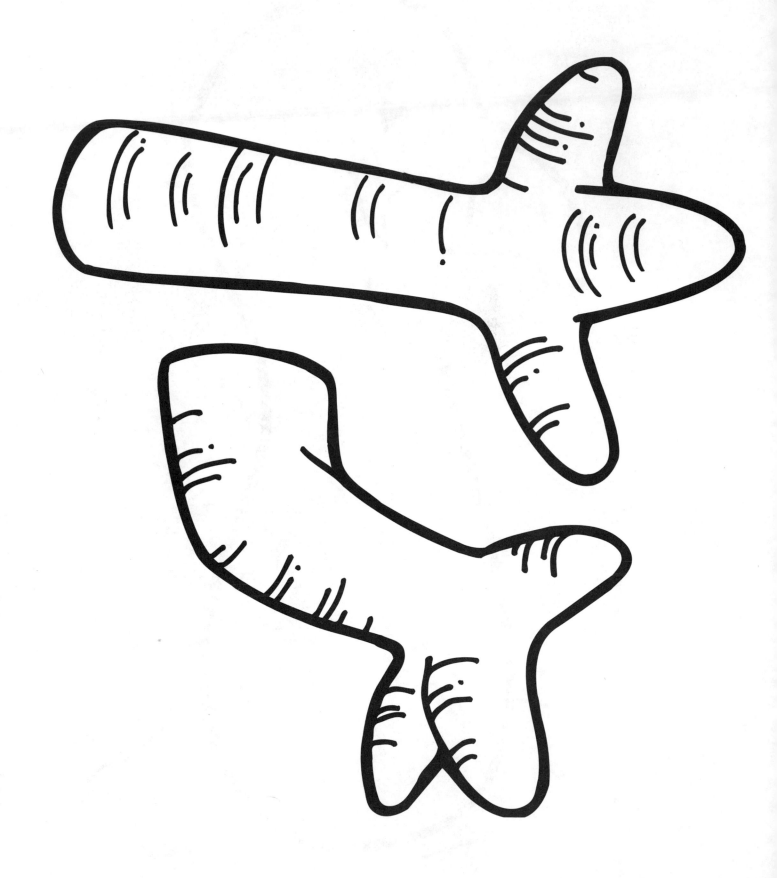

Name:

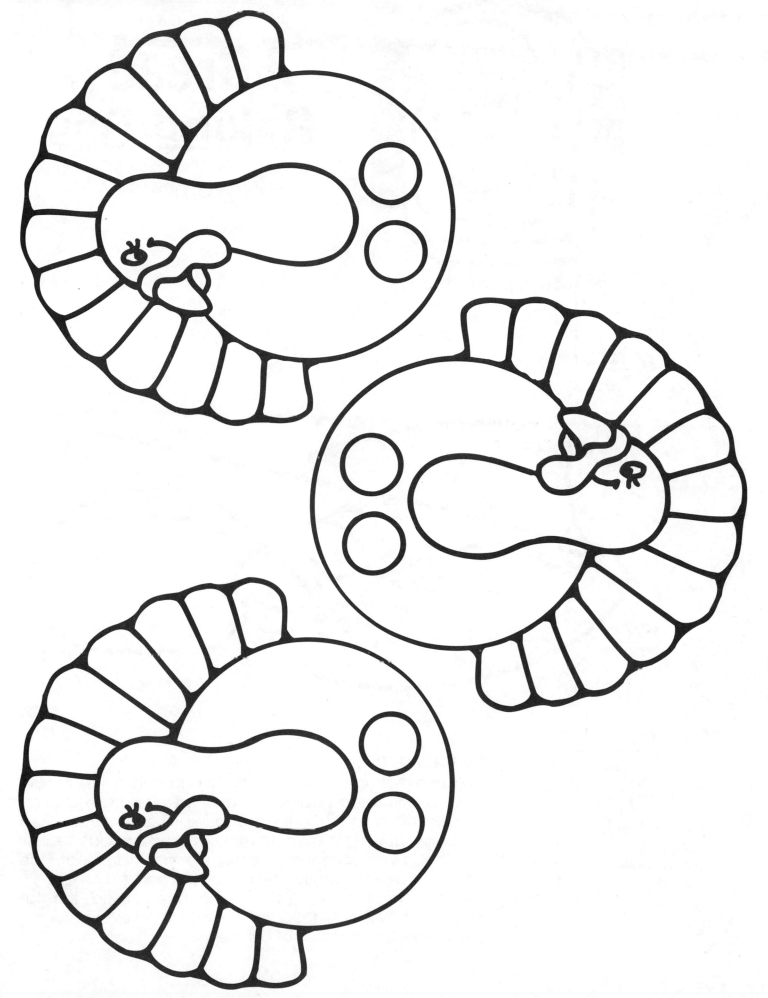

Bread Baking Day

November 17

Setting the Stage
• Display different types of bread from around the world.

Historical Background
People have been making bread from wheat and eating it for thousands of years. The first bread was simply crushed wheat mixed with water and baked into a flat pancake over a fire. Then in about 1000 BC yeast was first used in Egypt to make "raised" bread. Years later in Rome, bread was considered more important than meat. The government even baked bread for the people. Bread is such an important part of most of the world's diet, it has been called "the staff of life." Though we have more food choices now than ever before, bread continues to be a mainstay of our meals.

118

Literary Exploration

All About Bread by Geoffrey Patterson

The Bakers: A Simple Book About the Pleasures of Baking Bread by Jan Adkins

The Bakery Factory: Who Puts the Bread on Your Table by Aylette Jenness

Bread by David Glover

Bread by Dorothy Turner

Bread and Honey by Frank Asch

Bread and Jam for Frances by Russell Hoban

The Bread Book: All About Bread and How to Make It by Carolyn Meyer

Bread, Bread, Bread by Ann Morris

The Bread Dough Craft Book by Elyse Sommer

Bread Is for Eating by David and Phyllis Gershator

A Grain of Wheat: A Writer Begins by Clyde Bulla

Knead It, Punch It, Bake It by Judith Jones

The Little Red Hen by Paul Galdone

The Little Red Hen by Margot Zemach

A Loaf of Bread by Angela Lucas

Sanji and the Baker by Robin Tzannes and Korky Paul

Seven Loaves of Bread by Ferida Wolff

Stranger's Bread by Nancy Willard

This Is the Bread I Baked for Ned by Crescent Dragonwagon

Tony's Bread: An Italian Folktale by Tomie dePaola

When Batistine Made Bread by Treska Lindsey

Language Experience

• After reading *The Little Red Hen,* have students sequence the events to retell the story.

Writing Experience
• Let students write recipes for their favorite kinds of bread. See reproducible on page 125.

The recipe for my favorite kind of BREAD

FLOUR

SALT

YEAST YEAST

Name:

Math Experience
• Give students an opportunity to have "hands-on" practice with measuring before they make bread. Let them estimate equivalent measurements such as the amount of tablespoons in a cup or reinforce equivalent fractions. Provide measuring tools so they can check their estimates.

Science/Health Experience

- Create a science lesson around watching yeast rise. Explain that yeast is a plant and as it grows, it produces a gas. As the gas bubbles expand, the dough "rises."

Social Studies Experience

- After reading *The Bakers,* (a history of bread baking) make a time line using information from the book.

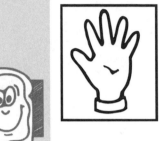

Music/Dramatic Experience

• Sing the nursery rhyme "Hot-Cross Buns."

> Hot-Cross Buns!
> Hot-Cross Buns!
> One a Penny,
> Two a Penny,
> Hot-Cross Buns!

• Act out the story "The Little Red Hen." Set page 123 for costume ideas.

Physical/Sensory Experience

⚠ Let students make homemade bread. For sanitary purposes, they can put their hands inside plastic sandwich bags to knead the bread.

Basic Bread Recipe

Add a package of yeast to warm water and a pinch of sugar. Set aside. In a large bowl, combine $2^1/2$ cups flour, $^1/3$ cup vegetable oil, $^1/3$ cup sugar and 1 T. salt. Mix with a mixer, then add the yeast mixture. Begin kneading the dough (about five minutes), then cover it. Punch down the dough when it has doubled in size. When it has doubled again, shape it into loaves and let it rise just above the loaf pans. Covered dough will rise in about an hour depending on the room temperature. Bake at 350°F. Two full-sized loaves will bake in about 30-35 minutes; small, individual loaves will bake in 10-12 minutes.

⚠ Gather bread recipes from other countries and let students try to make other types of bread. They can discover for themselves by taste, shape and texture how each differs.

Arts/Crafts Experience

⚠ Let students make sculptures with bread dough. *The Bread Dough Craft Book* by Elyse Sommer has a lot of ideas. Thaw frozen bread dough about five or six hours, then let students make creations or figures with the dough. The figures will stick together better if they are dipped in milk first. Brushing beaten egg over figures before baking will make a great glaze! Bake at 350°F for about 25 minutes.

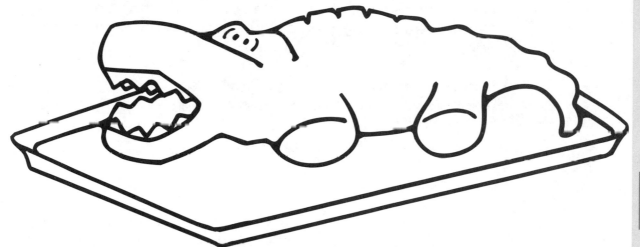

⚠ Let students make "bread paintings" by mixing food coloring with milk, then using cotton swabs to paint it directly on slices of bread.

• Challenge student to make "costumes" for the characters in the story of "The Little Red Hen" (pig snout, duck hat. chicken beak, etc.).
Suggestions:
The hen costume can be made from cutting/folding construction paper (like a cone shape for beak).
The duck costume can be made by decorating a baseball cap with permanent markers.
The pig snout can be made from an egg carton section fastened to string.

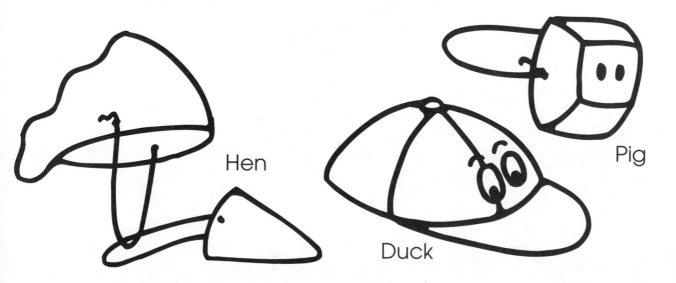

Hen

Duck

Pig

Extension Activities

- Students can bring favorite bread recipes from home to compile into a class recipe book.

- Visit a local bread bakery to see how bread is made.

⚠ To make breadsticks, thaw frozen bread dough and cut it lengthwise. Mix 1 beaten egg with 1/2-cup water to brush over breadsticks. Let the dough rise until double, then brush over it again. Sprinkle it with sesame seeds, Italian seasoning, coarse salt or parmesan cheese. Bake at 425°F for 10-12 minutes, then enjoy!

⚠ Host a bread-sampling party! Provide samples from various countries: German rye bread, French croissants, Irish scones, Middle Eastern pita bread, Russian pumpernickel bread, Mexican tortillas, U.S. sourdough bread and India's chapatti bread!

TLC10464 Copyright © Teaching & Learning Company, Carthage, IL 62321-0010

The recipe for my favorite kind of BREAD

Name:

Mickey Mouse's Birthday

November 18

Setting the Stage
• Display Disney memorabilia or books to engage students' interest.

Historical Background
Mickey Mouse made his debut in an animated cartoon called "Steamboat Willie," the first cartoon with sound, on this day in 1929, a month after the onset of The Great Depression. The inspiration for Mickey was provided by two real mice who scampered across Walt Disney's drawing board.

Literary Exploration
Disney's It's Magic! Stories from the Films by Todd Strasser
Mickey Mouse by Pierre Lambert
Mickey Mouse and Friends Movie Stories by Disney
Mickey Mouse Club Scrapbook by Keith Keller
The Mickey Mouse Magic Book by Disney
Mickey's Magnet by Franklyn Branley
Walt Disney's Mickey Mouse and His Boat by Alice Hughes
Walt Disney's Mickey Mouse and the Bicycle Race by Cindy West
Walt Disney's Mickey Mouse and the Peanuts by Cindy West
Walt Disney's Mickey Mouse and the Pet Shop by Mary Packard
Walt Disney's Mickey Mouse and the Pet Show by Joan Phillips

Language Experience

• Let students share experiences of visiting Disney theme parks.

Writing Experience

• Challenge each student to describe a new idea for a cartoon to submit to the Disney Corporation.

• Imagine that Disney creators run out of ideas and are looking for something new and exciting. Have students write their ideas for a new theme park ride at one of the Disney theme parks.

• Students will enjoy writing letters to Mickey about how he feels about being famous.

• See reproducible for writing activities on page 129.

Math Experience

• Draw large mouse-ear hats and write individual sums on the base of each hat. Students can brainstorm and write the addends or factors to equal each answer. (Example: Base 15, students might write a 10 on one ear and a 5 on the other.)

Mickey
Mouse

Mickey
Mouse

Mickey
Mouse

Music/Dramatic Experience

• Sing Mickey Mouse's theme song from the *Mickey Mouse Club*.

Arts/Crafts Experience

• Challenge students to create new comic strips featuring Mickey Mouse.

Extension Activities

• Write to the Mickey Mouse Club or Disney Corporation, asking for any Mickey Mouse memorabilia to be sent to your class through the mail.

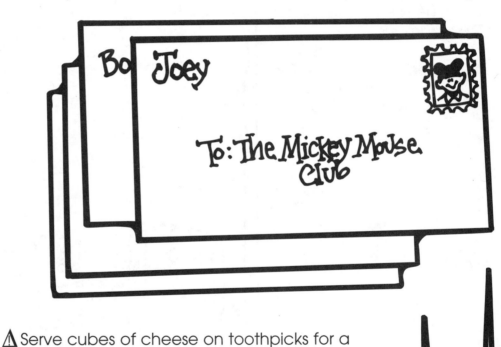

⚠ Serve cubes of cheese on toothpicks for a Mickey Mouse snack!

Follow-Up/Homework Idea

• Students can enjoy a favorite Mickey Mouse cartoon or Disney movie with their families.

National Smokeout Day

November 19

Setting the Stage
• Display anti-smoking, health-related posters from the American Cancer Society or local health facility to increase awareness of the dangers of tobacco.

Historical Background
Smoking was declared hazardous on this day in 1964. The American Cancer Society urges smokers to stop smoking for at least 24 hours today.

Literary Exploration
Kids and Smoking by Jamie Rattray
Know About Smoking by Margaret O. Hyde
Smoking by Judith Condon
Smoking by Lila Gano
Smoking by Sherry Sonnett
Smoking by Bonnie Szumski
Smoking and Health by Brian R. Ward
Smoking and You by Arnold Madison

Language Experience
• Debate the pros and cons of cigarettes and other products that may be considered unsafe or hazardous.

Writing Experience

- Let students describe their feelings about smoking. See reproducible on page 133.

Science/Health Experience

- Let students research the health-related risks of smoking, then share their findings with the class.

- Have them investigate "second-hand" smoke and its effects on non-smokers.

Smoking is:

Name:

Social Studies Experience

- Encourage students to find smokers who will commit to go 24 hours without smoking. Then let them interview the people to find out what the experience was like and what effect they think it will have on their future.

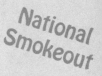

Music/Dramatic Experience

• Brainstorm what students can say or do when offered a cigarette. Let them form groups and role-play their ideas.

• Work together to create a musical jingle to warn people of the dangers of smoking.

Arts/Crafts Experience

• Students can create anti-smoking posters to put up around the school.

Extension Activities

• Invite someone in the health care field to bring items, posters and vital statistics about tobacco use to your class.

Values Education Experience

• Discuss peer pressure and how students can make wise decisions and responsible choices that will affect their future.

132

Name:

Pie Day

November 20

Setting the Stage

⚠ Set out a freshly baked pie and fill your room with its delicious aroma! Brainstorm descriptive words that the pie evokes. Later, after each student eats a piece, let them describe how it tastes, feels, etc.

Literary Exploration

Alligator Pie by Dennis Lee
A Apple Pie by Kate Greenaway
Apple Pie and Onions by Judith Caseley
The Blueberry Pie by Joy Cowley
The Cherry Pie Baby by Kay Chorao
Country Pie by Frank Asch
Easy as Pie: A Guessing Game of Sayings by Marcia Folsom
Ed Emberley's Picture Pie: A Circle Drawing Book by Edward Emberley
Elephant Pie by Hilda Offen
The Fabulous Principal Pie by James Hoffman
Gator Pie by Louise Mathews
How Do Octopi Eat Pizza Pie? Pizza Math by Time-Life Books
How Many Ways Can You Cut a Pie? by Jane Belk Moncure

Pie Day

Pie Day

Pie Day

Pie Day

TLC10464 Copyright © Teaching & Learning Company, Carthage, IL 62321-0010

Literary Exploration continued

How to Make a Mud Pie by Deborah Eaton
How to Make an Apple Pie and See the World by Marjorie Priceman
James Bear's Pie by Jim Latimer
Mud Pie: Food and Fun by Ngarangi Naden
Mud Pies by Judith Grey
Nobody Stole the Pie by Sonia Levitin
Pancake Pie by Sven Nordqvist
Operation Save the Teacher: Tuesday Night Pie by Meg Wolitzer
The Pie and the Patty Pan by Beatrix Potter
Pie in the Sky by Bruce Balan
Pie-Biter by Ruthanne McCunn
"Pie Problem" a poem from *Where the Sidewalk Ends* by Shel Silverstein
Piggie Pie! by Margie Palatini
Pollen Pie by Louise Argiroff
Richard Scarry's Pie Rats Ahoy! by Richard Scarry
Squash Pie by Wilson Gage
Tom Fox and the Apple Pie by Clyde Watson
"A" Was Once an Apple Pie by Edward Lear
Who Cried for Pie? by Veronica Buffington
Who Threw That Pie? by Robert Quackenbush

Language Experience

• With a pie shape, let students retell a story in sequence. They can divide the pie into fourths (or more) and retell through pictures and main ideas the four major events of the story.

Writing Experience

• After brainstorming words with descriptive imagery (about pies), let students write their favorite pie recipes to be compiled into a class pie cookbook. See reproducible on page 137.

My Favorite Pie

I like my pie cut round!

Name:

Math Experience

- After reading *Gator Pie*, introduce or review fractions.

- Let students practice simple fraction equivalents with pie pieces. See patterns on page 138.

Social Studies Experience

- Have students research some of the places mentioned in the book *How to Make an Apple Pie and See the World* by Marjorie Priceman.

Music/Dramatic Experience

- Let students pantomime or act out nursery rhymes such as "Simple Simon" or "Four and Twenty Blackbirds."

Physical/Sensory Experience

⚠ Have an old-fashioned pie-eating contest! Students put their hands behind their backs and eat pie (pudding and whipped cream in a pie tin) as quickly as they can until one finishes.

Arts/Crafts Experience

⚠ Finger-paint with pudding pies (pudding and whipped cream)! It's finger-licking good!

Extension Activities

⚠ Visit a bakery and watch them make pies. Then gather all the ingredients and make mini pies in class!

My Favorite Pie

I like my pie cut round!

Name:

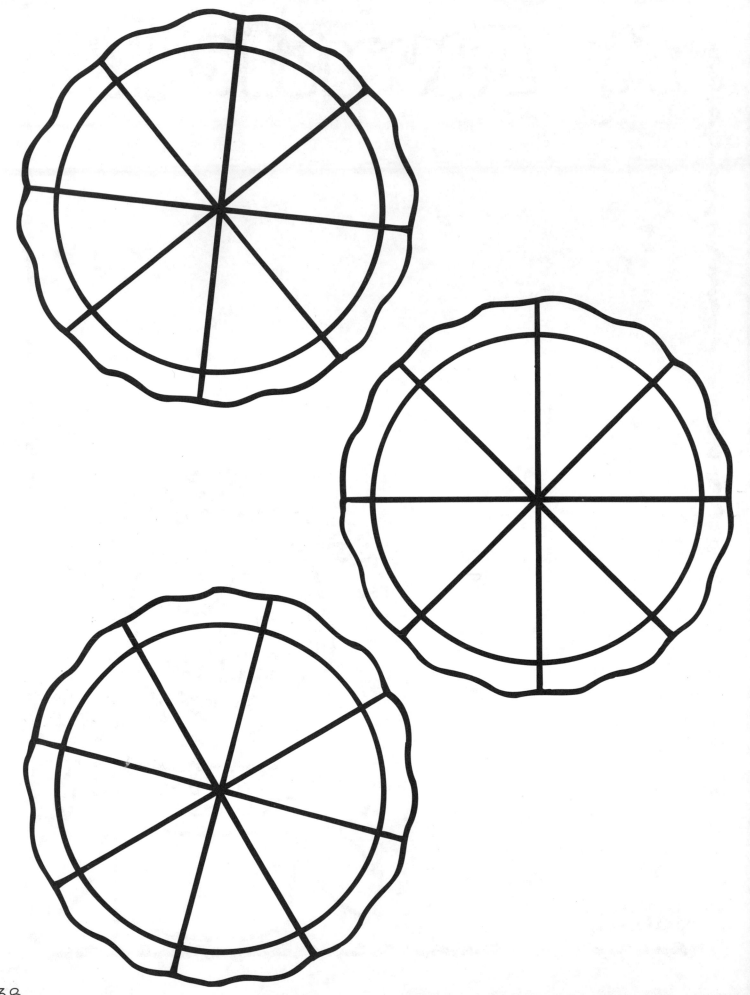

Thankful Hearts Day

November 21

Setting the Stage
- Display things for which to be thankful: books, flowers, pictures of family, etc.

Literary Exploration

Amelia Bedelia, Thank You by Peggy Parish
Giving Thanks by Chief Jake Swamp
I'm Thankful Every Day by P.K. Halinan
Say Thank You, Theodore by Wendy Lewison
Thank You by Janet Riehecky
Thanks by Ruth Shannon Odor

Language Experience

• Brainstorm reasons to be thankful, using words that begin with the letters in *thankful* or *thanksgiving*.

Writing Experience

• Have students write letters expressing thanks to those who have been helpful to them in some way.

• Encourage students to write booklets about what they are thankful for, adding a new page each day.

• Have a contest to see who can think of the most things he or she is thankful for.

• Let students draw a turkey by tracing around a hand. They can write something they are thankful for on each finger-shaped "feather."

• See reproducible for writing activities on page 142.

Arts/Crafts Experience

• Let students cut pictures from magazines and make collages of things they are thankful for.

Values Education Experience

• Discuss how gratitude is a valuable attitude.

Follow-Up/Homework Idea

• Encourage students to express appreciation for family members.

Name:

142

Important Day

November 22

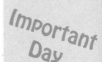

Setting the Stage

• Display student drawings on the three forms of matter (solids, liquids and gases) with the caption: "What MATTERS?"

Literary Exploration

About You . . . and Other Important People by Glen Griffin
The Important Book by Margaret Wise Brown
People Are Important by Eva Knox Evans
"The Schoolroom" from *Stuart Little,* Chapter 12, pages 92-98, by E.B. White
A Very Important Day by Maggie Rugg Herold

Language Experience
- Reinforce the "importance" of correct grammar, punctuation or similar language tools in communicating with others.

Writing Experience
- After reading *The Important Book* by Margaret Wise Brown, have students make their own individual "Important" books or make a class one with shared ideas.

Math Experience
- Have students work on monetary "values."

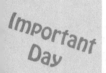

Science/Health Experience
- Begin a unit of science lessons on Forms of "Matter" (solids, liquids and gases).

Social Studies Experience
- Conduct a discussion on values (how they are determined, what strengthens or weakens them, how or if they change).

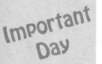

Music/Dramatic Experience
- Read Chapter 12 of "The Schoolroom," pages 92-98 of *Stuart Little* by E.B. White. Have a student act as Stuart Little, sitting on top of a desk to lead a discussion (as Stuart did) on what's important in life.

Arts/Crafts Experience

- Let students make Values Booklets. Copy pages 146-149 for each student. Have them write how they feel about each topic: "I really like . . . ," "I believe in . . . ," "I want to be known for . . . ," "Things that are really important to me are . . . ," "Something important that I have had to give up was . . . ."and "A personal symbol that represents me Is . . . ." They can compile the seven pages into a booklet. See reproducibles on pages 146-149.

- Have students write their favorite quotes with white chalk on black construction paper. Glue craft sticks around the edges for a "slate" border. (Suggestion: "The most important things in life are not things.")

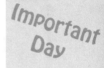

Values Education Experience

- Begin discussion about values and priorities that are important to us in our lives.

Follow-Up/Homework Idea

- Assign students to follow through with something important to them that they may have neglected lately (Examples: piano lessons or being responsible).

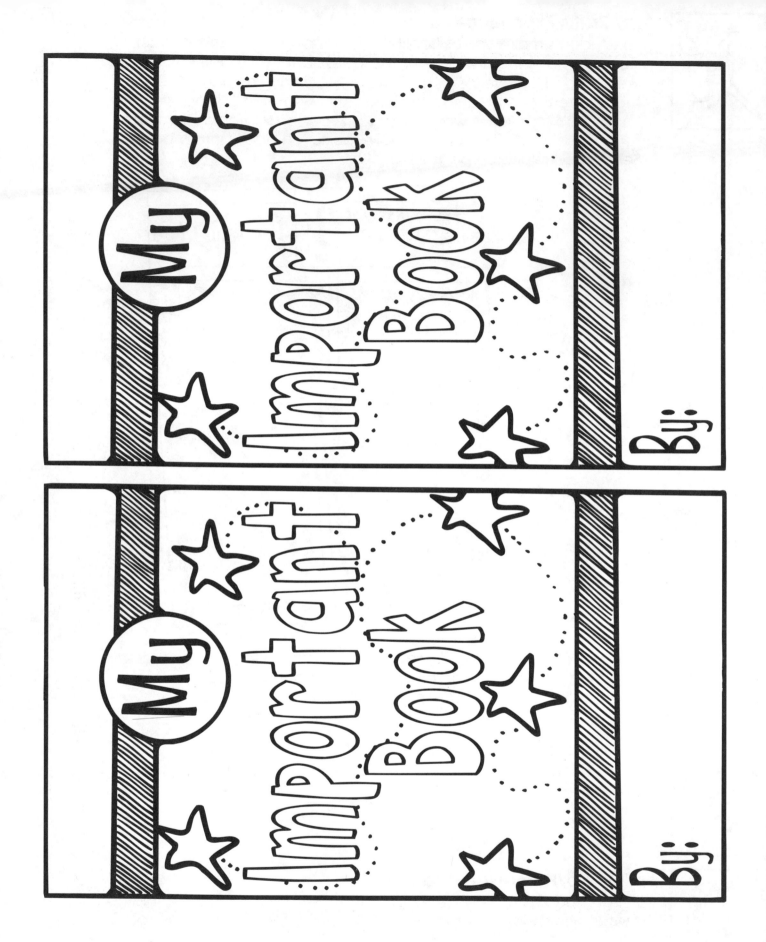

I really like . . .

I hope for . . .

Things that are really important to me are . . .

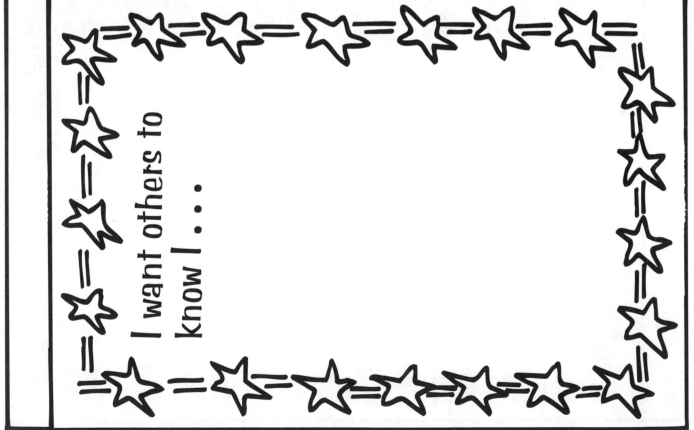

I want others to know I . . .

If you knew me, you would know I . . .

Something that was hard for me to give up was . . .

Family Day

November 23

Setting the Stage

- Display pictures of students' families on a bulletin board with the caption: "Many Families, Many Hours of Fun."

Literary Exploration

All Kinds of Families by Norma Simon
And Now We Are a Family by Judith Meredith
A Baby Sister for Frances by Russell Hoban
The Berenstain Bears and the Trouble with Grownups by Jan and Stan Berenstain
Big Sister, Little Brother by Terry Berger
Brothers Are All the Same by Mary Milgram
Christina Katerina and the Time She Quit the Family by Patricia Lee Gauch
Daddy by Jeannette Caines
The Dragon of an Ordinary Family by Margaret Mahy
Evan's Corner by Elizabeth Starr Hill
Families Are Different by Nina Pellegrini
Families Live Together by Esther K. Meeks
The Family by Seymour Rossel
Family by Ellie Simmons
Family Farm by Thomas Locker

Literary Exploration continued

Fudge-a-Mania (series) by Judy Blume
I Got a Family by Melrose Cooper
I'll Fix Anthony by Judith Viorst
Just Me and My Dad by Mercer Mayer
The Keeping Quilt by Patricia Polacco
Let's Find Out About the Family by Valerie Pitt
The Little Brute Family by Russell Hoban
My Brother Never Feeds the Cat by Reynold Ruffins
Nobody Asked Me if I Wanted a Baby Sister by Martha Alexander
Octopus Hug by Laurence Pringle
One More Thing, Dad by Susan Thompson
One of Three by Angela Johnson
On Mother's Lap by Ann Herbert Scott
Ramona Forever by Beverly Cleary
The Relatives Came by Cynthia Rylant
Superfudge (series) by Judy Blume
We're Very Good Friends, My Brother and I by P.K. Halinan
We're Very Good Friends, My Father and I by P.K. Halinan
We're Very Good Friends, My Mother and I by P.K. Halinan
We're Very Good Friends, My Sister and I by P.K. Halinan
Yonder by Tony Johnston
Your Family, My Family by Joan Drescher

Language Experience

• Let each student create a family tree or diagram of his or her family members. It may include just the immediate family or extend to grandparents if the student knows their names. Draw a simple family tree on the board to illustrate how to connect the individuals.

• Have each student print his or her family name vertically on a sheet of paper, then describe the family. (Example: BLAKE = B—Busy, L—Loud, A—Active, K—Kind, E—Enthusiastic) Display the family acrostics on the bulletin board display of students' family photographs (page 150).

• Challenge students to give reasons why their families should be given the Family of the Year award. Allow each student three to five minutes to champion his or her family to the rest of the group. When all the families have been represented, let each student design a Family of the Year certificate or award ribbon to take home to his or her family. (See Arts/Crafts Experience on page 154.)

Family
Day

Family
Day

Family
Day

Writing Experience

• Have each student interview a family member, asking questions about things they have always wanted to know about that person. Have them write down their findings.

• Let students write journal entries using one of these starter ideas:

My family likes to . . .
A funny thing happened in our family when . . .
My family likes the way I . . .
At our house, we . . .
I like to go home because . . .
I disappointed my parents when . . .
My parents were proud when . . .

• Give students five minutes to think of all the ways they feel thankful for their families. Have a contest to see who can make the longest list.

• See reproducible for writing activities on page 155.

Math Experience

• Begin a math lesson on fact "families."

• Give each student a budget with which to have a family party. Each needs to plan food, decorations, activities, etc., keeping an account of each item spent.

• Have students graph the age of each person in their families, including themselves on a bar graph.

• Review fractions by challenging students to use fractions to provide information about their families, such as: what fraction of the total family are in school, what fraction have jobs, what fraction have blue eyes, etc.

• Let each student try to figure the average age of the people in his or her family (by adding all the ages, then dividing the total by the number of family members).

Social Studies Experience

- Discuss what it means to be a member of a family.

- Brainstorm family projects or goals the families can work on together.

- Discuss how family life is different today than it was 100-150 years ago. To help student focus on life in those days read excerpts from a book such as *Little House in the Big Woods* or *Little House on the Prairie* by Laura Ingalls Wilder.

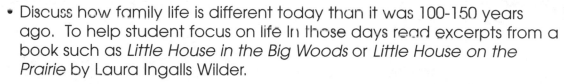

Music/Dramatic Experience

- Let students role-play family members (father, mother, sister, brother or grandmother).

- Write a song about families to a familiar tune such as "The Farmer in the Dell." Work together on it, with every body making suggestions. Then sing it together.
  Example: Families are fun,
  Families are fun.
  We all live together
  and love everyone.

Physical/Sensory Experience

- Challenge students to invent games for their families to play together.

- Play Please Clean Your Room! Divide the class in two groups. Have one group stand on one side of the room with the second group on the other. Decide on a specific dividing line, with each group staying on their own side. Crumple up large wads of paper for both groups. When you say, "Please clean your room!" each group scrambles to clean up their side by throwing the trash to the other side. At the sound of a whistle, everyone freezes and the side with the least amount of trash, wins.

- "Mother, May I?" is a game children love to play. Introduce them to this new version. Line them up against a wall. Stand against the opposite wall. Challenge them with family statements to get them to move (if there are three children in your family, take two giant steps forward). They must say, "Mother, may I?" then move if the statement describes their family. (Other suggestions: where they live, a baby in your family, hair color, eye color, car, job, etc.)

Arts/Crafts Experience

- Have students design family flags to fly when someone in their family is being honored.

- Students can design T-shirts with the family name on them. Perhaps they can encourage their families to have some professionally made to wear at the next family reunion.

- Divide your class into small groups to design and make small houses from craft sticks. They can also make family member puppets out of craft sticks.

- Let each student design a certificate or award ribbon to give to his or her family for being "The Family of the Year."

Extension Activities

- Begin "spotlighting" families in your class. Each week invite members of a student's family to visit and tell about themselves.

- Discuss how family members sometimes move away from one another when they get older and don't see one another as often as they'd like. Take some (or all) of your students to visit a nursing home to be "stand-in families" for residents who don't get many visitors.

Values Education Experience

- Invite students to share feelings about the importance of each member of a family and tell what they mean to each other.

Follow-Up/Homework Idea

- Encourage students to invite their families to take a family walk together or begin a family project.

Name: _____

Game and Puzzle Day

November 24

Setting the Stage

- Invite children to bring games and puzzle books to class. Stack them under a bulletin board. Across the board place the caption: "We're Game for Anything!" Around the caption mount playing cards on which you have taped school pictures of the students in your class.

Historical Background

People have enjoyed playing games of various kinds since before history was written down. As far back as 3000 b.c. Egyptians were playing a game called Senet. In 1400 board games were being used in Egypt. Around 700 b.c. people began playing games with dice. Backgammon was popular in the Babylonian Empire in the fourth century. Chess was played in India in the eighth century and in the thirteenth century, Indians played an early version of Snakes and Ladders. The popular game of checkers probably began in the sixteenth century. By the 1700s people were playing card games such as Solitaire. In 1933 the board game Monopoly™ was invented and in 1947 Scrabble™ was introduced.

Literary Exploration

38 Ways to Entertain Your Grandparents by Dette Hunter and Deirdre Betteridge
52 Fun Family Games by Lynn Gordon
Amazing Game Board Book (Innovative Kids)
Game for a Game? by Robynne Eagan
Games by Meryl Doney
Indoor Games That Teach by Robynne Eagan
Lu & Clancy's Secret Codes by Adrian Mason and Pat Cupples
Sidewalk Games by Glen Vecchione

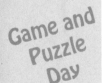

Language Experience

- Let students study some of the game boxes at the bulletin board display to see the kinds of words used to describe the games and make people want to play them. Then let them imagine that they work for a company that produces games. Have them brainstorm words to advertise their games. List the words on the board. Challenge students to pick out the adjectives (which most of the words should be).

- Let students create crossword puzzles or word search puzzles, then trade them to see if they can solve each other's puzzles.

Writing Experience

- Read the how-to-play directions from a well-known game. Then have each student write step-by-step directions for how to play a favorite game.

- Let students write a story or essay using one of these starter ideas:
  My family always enjoys playing . . .
  The first game I learned to play was . . .
  Families should play more games together because . . .
  The best game player at our house is . . .

- Challenge students to imagine themselves as champion game players who have been challenged by a player from another country. They should write about what happens when they represent their country and try to beat the foreign challenger. Who wins? How? What happens?

Math Experience

- Let students choose math partners to compete in a game of Concentration to review addition and subtraction facts. Copy page 159 for each pair of students. Have them cut out the cards, scramble them, and lay them facedown, then take turns turning over two cards at a time. When a student uncovers a problem and answer that match, the two cards are taken out of play and put aside as points for that student. See 159 for Concentration cards.

- Divide students into pairs to review math facts with playing cards. Each student puts down two number cards and they take turns adding, subtracting or multiplying the numbers. This game can also be played by rolling dice or with dominoes.

Social Studies Experience

- Challenge students to find out about the games children play in foreign countries. They can look in picture books and encyclopedias to find information about each country they're interested in. Play some of the games they discover.

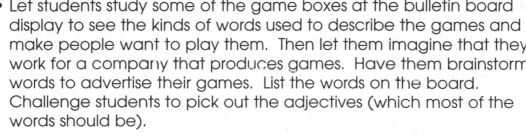
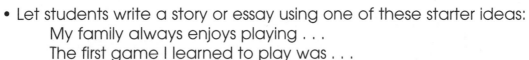

Music/Dramatic Experience

- Divide students into two teams and play a game of Charades. Before class write book titles, TV shows and film titles on slips of paper for them to use.

Physical/Sensory Experience

- Have each student write down one item to be found on a scavenger hunt in the school yard. Compile the items into a list and make copies. Divide students into two to four teams and give each a list. Give them boundaries beyond which they may not go to find the items on the list, then let them go. (You may want to appoint an adult to oversee each team, but not help.) Blow a whistle when time is up and see which team found the most items on the list.

Arts/Crafts Experience

- Challenge each student to use his or her creativity to design a new box cover or advertisement for a popular game.

- Let students design new games with game pieces, game boards and spinners to determine how far to move. They can take their completed games home to play with their families.

Extension Activities

- Challenge another class to compete with your students in a game of Stand-Up Tic-Tac-Toe. Use masking tape to create tic-tac-toe squares on the floor. Have your students help you make large poster board Xs and Os for players to wear. Prepare questions for players to answer. If a student answers correctly, he puts on an X or O and goes to stand on the square he chooses. You might want to make this a regular rainy day event!

Values Education Experience

- The Saturday through the Sunday of Thanksgiving week each year is celebrated as National Game and Puzzle Week. Explain to your students that this was done to encourage families to spend time together playing games and doing puzzles. Talk about the importance of families spending time together. Let students share some good times they have had with their families.

Follow-Up/Homework Idea

- Encourage students to turn everyday things into games and puzzles. (Example: See how many stop signs or blue cars they can count on the walk or bus ride home.)

$8 + 8$	16	$12 - 4$	8
$5 + 4$	9	$10 - 5$	5
$6 + 6$	12	$7 - 4$	3
$9 + 6$	15	$5 - 3$	2

Thanksgiving Day

November 25
(varies)

Historical Background

This day was proclaimed by Governor William Bradford as a day of thanksgiving after the Pilgrims settled in the New World. Although Thanksgiving has been celebrated since then on various dates, a woman named Sara Josepha Hale suggested it be a national holiday. Her idea was approved by President Abraham Lincoln, who made the last Thursday of every November our official Thanksgiving Day.

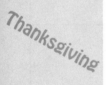

Literary Exploration

Arthur's Thanksgiving by Marc Brown
The First Thanksgiving Feast by Joan Anderson
Harvest Feast by Wilhelmina Harper
How Many Days to America? A Thanksgiving Story by Eve Bunting
One Tough Turkey: A Thanksgiving Story by Steven Kroll
The Purple Turkey and Other Thanksgiving Stories by David A. Adler
Thanksgiving Day by Gail Gibbons
Thanksgiving Feast and Festival by Mildred Lockhardt
Tiny Turtle's Thanksgiving by Dave Ross
Today Is Thanksgiving by P.K. Halinan
A Turkey for Thanksgiving by Eve Bunting

Language Experience

• Invite students to share some of their favorite family memories or traditions.

160

Language Experience continued

- Create a classroom Thanksgiving Cookbook! Invite each student to tell you the recipe from memory of a favorite Thanksgiving dish. Type these and assemble them in a cookbook to give parents for a Thanksgiving gift. See reproducibles on pages 165-166.

Writing Experience

- Have students brainstorm creative uses for Thanksgiving leftovers (Examples: cranberry critters, plum pudding play dough).

- Let students share their favorite Thanksgiving traditions or memories, then write about them.

- Have students describe the senses (smells, sights, tastes) of Thanksgiving dinner. Encourage them to use sensory imagery ("the delicious smell of buttery turkey" or the "sick feeling of having eaten too much").

- Invite students to write about what the perfect Thanksgiving would be for them.

- Have students imagine a Thanksgiving in another period of time (such as the Civil War) and write about it.

- See reproducible for writing activities on page 167.

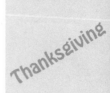

Writing Experience continued

- After sharing traditions and memories, let students write about traditions that they would like to begin with their families when they grow up. See reproducible on page 168.

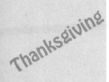

Math Experience

- Give each student play money with which to buy items for Thanksgiving dinner. Have them keep a record to account for each item and its price.

- Describe this scenario: The number of guests expected for Thanksgiving dinner has doubled, so now each recipe will need to be doubled. Give sample recipes and have them double the measurements. (Example: $1/4$ cup sugar becomes $1/2$ cup sugar.)

- The day after Thanksgiving is typically the busiest shopping day of the year. Have students calculate how many shopping days are left until Christmas.

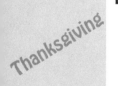

162

Science/Health Experience

- Reinforce personal hygiene before meals, such as: washing hands when preparing food and personal safety when using kitchen tools and utensils.

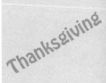

Social Studies Experience

- Learn about the history of the first Thanksgiving. Talk about how cooking preparations today are different from that first Thanksgiving.

Music/Dramatic Experience

- Have students act out the first Thanksgiving. Use costumes made in Pilgrims' Pride Day or Wampum Day (pages 24-25, 77).

- Sing a Thanksgiving song to the tune of "B-I-N-G-O." Make it up as you go. (Example: "F-E-A-S-T F-E-A-S-T F-E-A-S-T. Our tummy's will be full!")

Physical/Sensory Experience

• Engage students in fitness activities (run around the school yard, jumping jacks, etc.) to work off that sluggish feeling after a feast.

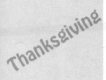

Arts/Crafts Experience

• Let students design table settings and place mats for the Thanksgiving feast. Decorated construction paper can become a place mat. A portion of a decorated toilet paper tube can be a napkin ring. A paper cup with feathers on the back and a turkey on the front can be a cup holder. A handwritten name on a folded piece of paper can be a name card.

• Have students draw a mural of what they expect their Thanksgiving meals to be.

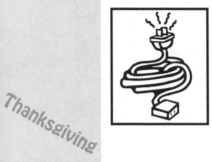

Extension Activities

⚠ Have a class Thanksgiving feast! Enlist parents to bring menu items (cornbread, popcorn, fruit salad, beef jerky, apple juice). After students act out the Thanksgiving story, everyone eats! (A pilgrim stew with vegetables from each student can be a stress-less feast!)

⚠ Let students make miniature cornucopias out of sugar ice cream cones and fill them with a treat such as candies, trail mix or nuts. To make the sugar cones curl like a cornucopia, hold them over steam.

⚠ Show students how to make even smaller cornucopias by placing Trix™ cereal (fruit) pieces into Bugles™ corn snacks. Fasten them on vanilla wafers with white frosting.

• Encourage your students to give to others. Contact a local agency and have students contribute food items to provide Thanksgiving dinner for a needy family.

Follow-Up/Homework Idea

• Encourage students to eat all their vegetables before their pumpkin pie on Thanksgiving Day!

Recipe for: _____

By: _____

Recipe for: _____

By: _____

Name:

THANKSGIVING TRADITIONS

Name:

Charles Schulz's Birthday

November 26

Setting the Stage

• Display *Peanuts* gang cartoon figures and books.

Historical Background

Charles Schulz, cartoonist and creator of the *Peanuts* gang, was born on this day in 1922.

Literary Exploration

Peanuts (series) by Charles M. Schulz

Language Experience

• Review sequencing events with *Peanuts* cartoons. Cut off the last cartoon square and have students predict the ending.

Writing Experience

• Let students cut out *Peanuts* pictures from some of the cartoons, then paste them on white paper in another order. Let them write new dialogue for the *Peanuts* characters.

• Challenge students to write from the point of view of the underdog, Charlie Brown, about how they think he feels.

Math Experience

• Have students bring in their favorite cartoons. Tally the results and show them on a class graph to determine the most popular ones.

Social Studies Experience

• In 1754, Benjamin Franklin designed the first comic strip for his newspaper, *The Pennsylvania Gazette*. The cartoon showed a snake cut into 13 pieces (representing the 13 colonies). Discuss how comic strips have evolved over the years. Have they changed much?

Arts/Crafts Experience

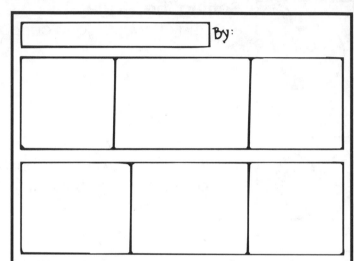

• Have students design birthday cards for Charles Schulz.

• Challenge students to try their hand at cartooning. See the comic strip reproducible on page 171.

Extension Activities

• Try cooperative cartooning. Divide the class into cooperative learning groups, with a designated member to lead each group. Each group member should be responsible for one task: gather ideas, draw, write dialogue, share the cartoon with the whole group.

⚠ Serve peanuts or Red Baron® (Snoopy's rival) Pizza slices for a snack.

Follow-Up/Homework Idea

• Encourage students to watch a favorite Snoopy or Charlie Brown video with their families.

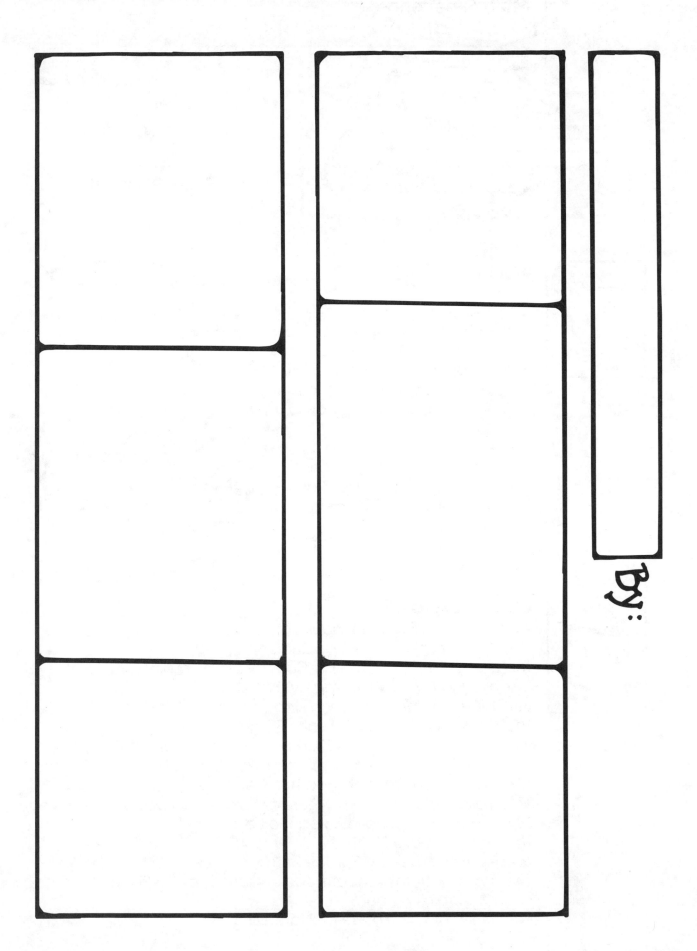

By:

Thinking Day

November 27

Setting the Stage

- Begin a tradition of starting each morning with a brain buster trivia challenge. (Example: Think of things that roll.) Write the challenge on the board or leave it on desks for students to work on to do independently or as a class.

- Put trivia or brain buster challenges in an old fish bowl or tank. Call it your classroom Think Tank.

Literary Exploration

About Your Brain by Seymour Simon
The Book of Think by Marilyn Burns
The Brain: What It Is, What It Does by Ruth Dowling Bruun, et al
Discovering Positive Thinking by Rita Milios
Every Kid's Guide to Thinking and Learning by Joy Berry
The Great Brain (series) by John Fitzgerald
If I Were in Charge of the World and Other Worries by Judith Viorst
The Kid's Book of Brain Bogglers by T. S. Burroughs
Look Inside Your Brain by Heather Alexander, et al
"The Loser" a poem from *Where the Sidewalk Ends* by Shel Silverstein
My Name Is Brain Brian by Jeanne Betancourt
Thinking by Kathie Smith
The Thinking Place by Barbara Joosse
The Turn About, Think About, Look About Book by Beau Gardner
Use Your Brain by Paul Showers
Your Busy Brain by Louise McNamara

172

Language Experience

• Challenge students with some brain-busting activities: Give them items to recall within a sequence (serialization), have them identify common characteristics within a group of objects (classification) or let them follow a sequence of events and retrace them back to the beginning (reversibility).

Writing Experience

• Invite students to write their own books with a clear beginning, middle and end. They should have a consistent main idea that flows throughout the book with supporting details. After they have gone through the editing process, let them illustrate and prepare their books for "publishing." Take them to a local copy shop for binding. Let students share their books with the class, then keep the books in your classroom library for others to read at free time.

Math Experience

• Involve students in writing their own math story problems. They should think of everyday problem-solving activities that they do. Have them trade with other students to solve the problems. The author of each story problem can be the "teacher" and correct the other student's work.

Science/Health Experience

• Study the brain and its functions.

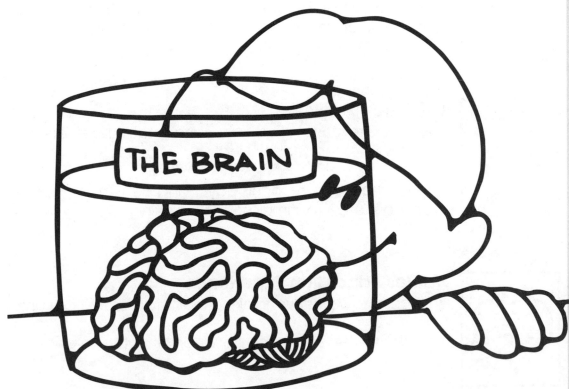

Social Studies Experience

- Discuss the importance of creative and original thought.

- Talk about what it means when people say, "Think BIG!"

- Give a list of miscellaneous answers, and let students come up with possible questions to fit the answers.

Music/Dramatic Experience

- Have students change a familiar story or song (with enough of its originality to make it recognizable) then share it with the class. See if others recognize its original form.

Physical/Sensory Experience

- Challenge students to put on their "thinking caps" and design a new game, with rules and directions for everyone to play.

Arts/Crafts Experience

- Make flip-top heads to encourage positive thinking! Provide head shapes for students to decorate. Then have them cut off the top of each head (where the brain would be located) and add a matching shape on which they have written positive thoughts. (Example: "I am beautiful and capable!") Over the positive thought, they staple the original top of the head with the hair on the outside and the positive thoughts on the inside. The head can be flipped up to show the positive thoughts in the brain.

Extension Activities

- Host a Great Brain Festival! Have rotating centers of activities that promote extended thinking!

⚠ To add a little fun on this day, hand out "brain food" (nuts, raisins, pretzels, etc.) to stimulate their thinking!

Values Education Experience

- Discuss how positive thinking leads to positive actions.

- Evaluate the difference between knowledge and wisdom.

Spots and Dots Day

November 28

Setting the Stage

- Wear clothes that have lots of spots or dots and invite your class to do the same.

- Reinforce the idea of looking for the good in others by hanging up a sheet of paper on the wall or door on which you have written the caption: "I SPOTTED Something Really Nice Today!" Challenge students to catch each other doing acts of kindness and nice things so they can write them on the sign.

Literary Exploration

Dots and Spots by Carol Morley
Dots, Spots, Speckles and Stripes by Tana Hoban
Freckle Juice by Judy Blume
How the Guinea Fowl Got Her Spots by Barbara Knutson
How the Leopard Got His Spots by Rudyard Kipling
Itchy, Itchy Chicken Pox by Grace Maccarone
McSpot's Hidden Spots: A Puppyhood Secret by Laura Seeley
Ms. Blanche, the Spotless Cow by Zidrou
Oscar's Spots by Janet Robertson
Put Me in the Zoo by Robert Lopshire
Spots, Feathers and Curly Tails by Nancy Tafuri
Ten Black Dots by Donald Crews
The Three Dots by Elise Primavera
What Has Spots? by Jackie Goodyear
Where's Spot? by Eric Hill

Language Experience

- Reinforce the skill of categorizing by having students see how many similarities they can "spot" (blends, compound words, adjectives, etc.).

- This is a great opportunity to reinforce punctuation with periods or colons, etc.

- Have students brainstorm everything they can think of that has spots or dots!

Writing Experience

- Have students write about experiences when they were really in a tough "spot." See reproducible on page 180.

- Let students play "teacher" trying to "spot" any mistakes as they proofread their own writing assignment.

Math Experience

- Let students play math games involving dice or dots (such as dominoes) to count or add. See dice pattern on page 181.

⚠ Attach paper pull-off dot stickers to students' hands and arms and let them count the dots or add the dots on two or three students.

Math Experience continued

- Do "dot-to-dot" counting by numbers such as fives.

- Cut paper plates in half. On one half draw dots. Put the number on the other half of the paper plate. Make several, then mix them up and see if students can make equivalent matches.

- Play Bingo with round candies. Have students write numbers on cards divided into Bingo squares. List number possibilities on the board and let students choose which numbers to put where on their cards. Call out math problems, such as 6 + 8 or 5 x 5. Students find the answers on their cards and cover them with round candies. The first person with a Bingo line wins!

Science/Health Experience

- Investigate how diseases such as "spotted" fever, measles and chicken pox are passed around.

Social Studies Experience

- "Spot"light students' good qualities by highlighting them one at a time. Have classmates suggest strengths and good qualities individuals have that make them unique and special.

Music/Dramatic Experience

- Borrow the school "spot"light and let students ham it up with a talent or two.

Physical/Sensory Experience

• Play the game, Tiddlywinks.

• Let students play a game of tossing coins into hoops.

• Play Pin the Spot on the Dalmatian. See pattern on page 182.

Arts/Crafts Experience

• Learn about Seurat's unique art style called Pointillism. Students can dip Q-tips™ into tempera paint and make outlines of tiny dots to form pictures. They can fill in the designs with many other little dots.

• Let each student make a dot-to-dot picture for another student to complete.

⚠ Students will enjoy making necklaces out of "O"-shaped cereal.

• Work with students to make papier-mâché ladybugs or spotted leopards.

178

Extension Activities

- Try to find some spots candy (candy dots on paper strips) for students to eat.

⚠ Serve pizza with pepperoni polka dots!

⚠ Give students sugar cookies, icing and colored sprinkle dots or round candies. Let them be creative in making designs on their cookies!

Values Education Experience

- Brainstorm problem-solving situations where students find themselves in a "rough spot." (Examples: someone offers them drugs, they lose their house key or a bully picks a fight) Dramatize some options to help them out of sticky situations.

My Tough SPOT

Name:

182

Louisa May Alcott's Birthday

November 29

Setting the Stage

• Display some of Louisa May Alcott's books to engage interest.

Little Women

Eight Cousins

Little Men

Historical Background

Louisa May Alcott was an American author born on this day in 1832. She wrote the classic tale, *Little Women*.

Literary Exploration

Eight Cousins by Louisa May Alcott
Invincible Louisa by Cornelia Meigs
Jo's Boys by Louisa May Alcott
Little Men by Louisa May Alcott
Little Women by Louisa May Alcott
Louisa May Alcott by Kathleen Burke
Louisa May Alcott: Author, Nurse, Suffragette by Carol Greene
Louisa May Alcott: Her Girlhood Diary by Louisa May Alcott

Language Experience

- Discuss what Louisa May Alcott may have meant when she said, "That is a good book it seems to me, which is opened with expectation and closed with profit." Ask students what they think she would have considered a good book.

Writing Experience

- Louisa May Alcott was a prolific journal writer who got many of her ideas for books from her journals. Have students begin writing in personal journals. Provide little notebooks to get them started or have them make their own. See reproducible on page 186.

- Louisa wrote about many adventures she had with her family in Concord, Massachusetts. Have students write about one of their family adventures.

Social Studies Experience

• Louisa May Alcott was a friend of Ralph Waldo Emerson and Henry David Thoreau. Nathaniel Hawthorne was also a neighbor. All three were important writers. Ask students how they think they influenced Alcott's writing. If they could pick three specific people to be their friend or neighbor, who would they be?

Music/Dramatic Experience

• When Louisa was 13 years old, she wrote her first play. Let students form groups and try writing short plays.

Arts/Crafts Experience

• Let students decorate the cover of their own journals.

Louisa
May
Alcott

Extension Activities

⚠ Try a recipe from Gretchen Anderson, a nine-year-old inspired by Louisa May Alcott's books. Gretchen researched many 19th century cookbooks and chose recipes from that time period (such as gingerbread and baked apples). Her cookbook is called, *The Louisa May Alcott Cookbook.*

• Are there any before-the-turn-of-the-century homes in your area? Try to schedule your class for a visit.

Values Education Experience

• Discuss how family life has changed since the time of Louisa May Alcott. Are we more or less busy? Do we spend more or less time together? How have values changed or been maintained?

Louisa
May
Alcott

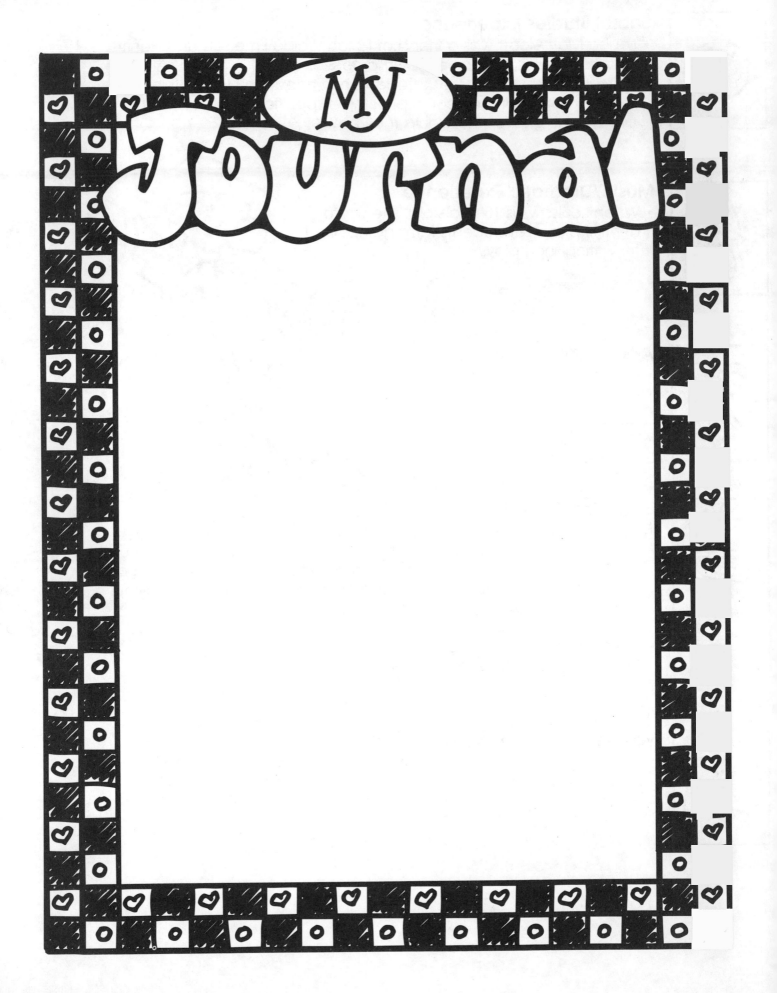

Mark Twain's Birthday

November 30

Setting the Stage
- Display common playthings from the 19th century (for example, a slingshot or marbles. Dress up in overalls and a straw hat.

Historical Background
This American writer (his real name was Samuel Clemens) was born on this day in 1835. He spent his early years as a printer, then a Mississippi river pilot and then a writer.

Literary Exploration
Adventures of Huckleberry Finn by Mark Twain
The Adventures of Tom Sawyer by Mark Twain
America's Mark Twain by May McNeer
The Importance of Mark Twain by Skip Press
Life on the Mississippi by Mark Twain
Mark Twain, Boy of Old Missouri by Miriam Mason
Mark Twain, What Kind of Name Is That? by
　　Robert Quackenbush
Mark Twain: Author of Tom Sawyer by Carol
　　Greene
Mark Twain: The Story of Samuel Clemens by
　　Jim Hargrove
River Boy: The Story of Mark Twain by William Anderson
Young Mark Twain by Louis Sabin
Young Mark Twain and the Mississippi by Harnett Thomas Kane

Language Experience

- Play the Clothesline Game (a variation of Hangman with clothes hung on a line). Use letters to see if the class can figure out Mark Twain's given name (_am_e_ _ _em_ _ _).

S _ _ _ _ _ _ _ _ L _ _ _ _ N _

- Mark Twain once said, "The man who does not read good books has no advantage over the man who can't read them." Use his quote to begin a discussion on what students think makes a good book.

- Read about the adventures of Huck Finn or Tom Sawyer. Have students compare and contrast how the tricks they used to play are different or similar to those that children play today.

- Challenge students to spell *Mississippi*.

Writing Experience

- Have students write about times they did something they shouldn't have. "I knew I was in trouble when . . . ." See reproducible on page 191.

Social Studies Experience

- Students can research travel by steamboat and compare it with travel today. Have them make a time line to show the evolution of travel from Twain's time to now.

Music/Dramatic Experience

- Let students form groups and act out scenes from *The Adventures of Tom Sawyer* and *Adventures of Huckleberry Finn*.

Physical/Sensory Experience

- Students will enjoy playing Tom Sawyer-type games such as: thumb wrestling, a taffy pull and wheelbarrow or sack races.

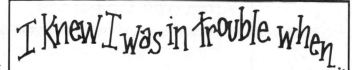
I knew I was in trouble when...

Name:

Mark Twain

Mark Twain

Mark Twain

Arts/Crafts Experience

• Have a Tom Sawyer picket fence painting contest! Have each student paint a small area of a fence drawn on a large piece of paper. Set a timer for one or two minutes and let them go! Later, they can paint more leisurely and add details such as knotholes.

Values Education Experience

• Mark Twain said, "Kindness is a language which the deaf can hear and the blind can read." Brainstorm with your students some acts of kindness they could exhibit today that others can hear and read.

• Twain said, "If you tell the truth, you don't have to remember anything." Let students discuss in small groups what that means to them, then report to the class.

I Knew I was in trouble when...

Name:

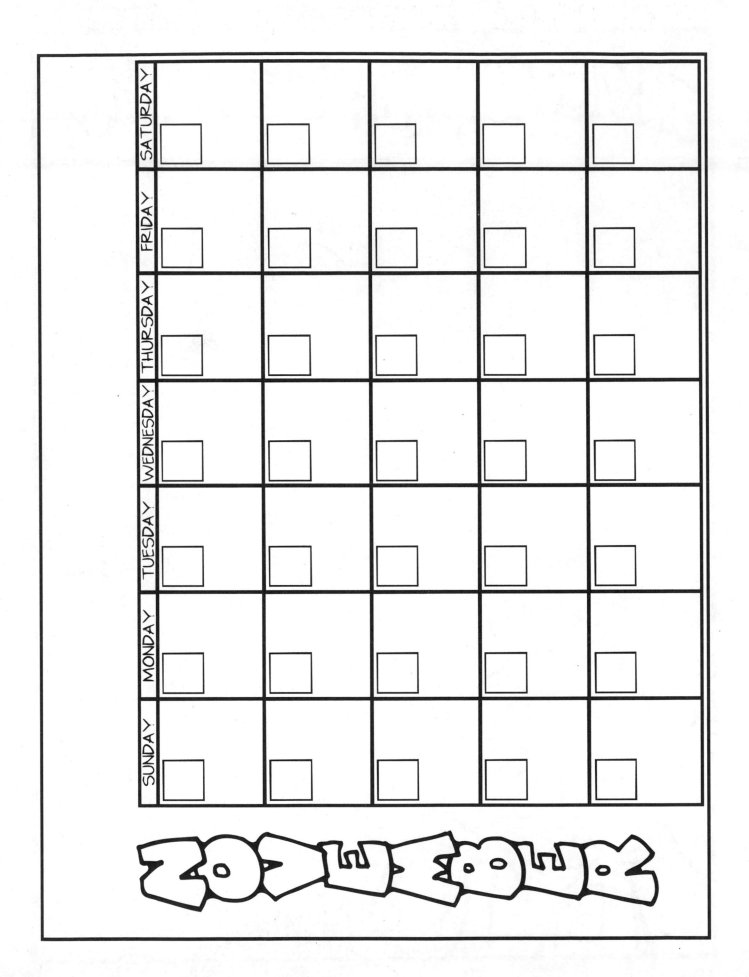